ONCE UPON A QUILT

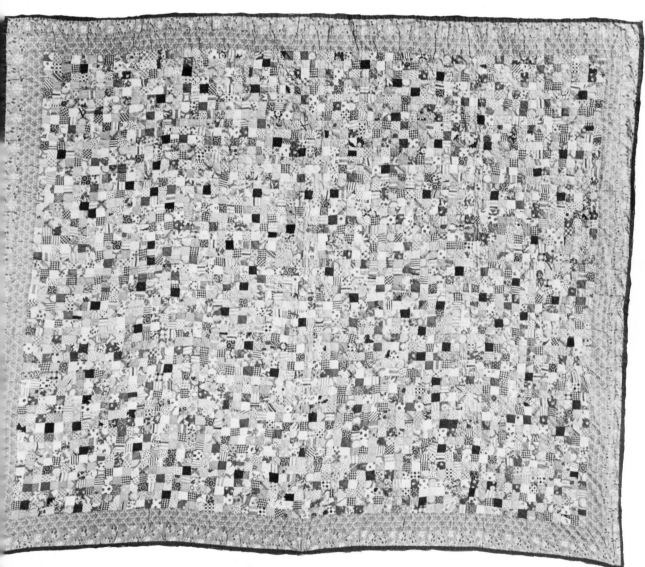

OSTAGE STAMP, 1900
anchester, Maryland
ade by Sarah J. Hann (Author's Collection)

ONCE UPON A QUILT

patchwork design & technique

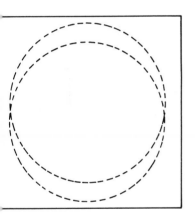
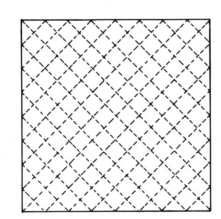
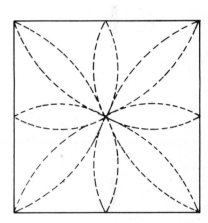

Celine Blanchard Mahler

VNR VAN NOSTRAND REINHOLD COMPANY
New York Cincinnati Toronto London Melbourne

Dedicated to the memory of my precious
mother, Agnes, who gave me life,
and to Marty, who gave me love

To Mamie and Frank Galt, who gave me
incentive, to Nat and Lucille Cohen, who
gave me direction, and to Nancy Newman,
who gave me editorial help, my deepest
thanks. To Mauve Greenbaum, who
researched for endless hours, shared her
quilting experiences with me, and made the
samples in this book, I am forever indebted.

Frontispiece:
Detail of Crazy Quilt, 1886. Note date and embroidery work.
(Courtesy of Joan Kindler, Whitestone, New York)

Van Nostrand Reinhold Company Regional Offices:
New York   Cincinnati   Chicago   Millbrae   Dallas
Van Nostrand Reinhold Company International Offices:
London   Toronto   Melbourne
Copyright © 1973 by Litton Educational Publishing, Inc.
Library of Congress Catalog Card Number 73-3943
ISBN 0-442-24966-7 (Paper)
ISBN 0-442-24967-5 (Cloth)
Designed by Rosa Delia Vasquez
Color photographs and photographs on pages
30, 33, 43, 46, 82, 84, 86, 94
by Richard Luria
Remaining photographs by Dennis Purse
Published by Van Nostrand Reinhold Company
450 West 33rd Street, New York, N.Y. 10001
5 7 9 11 13 15 16 14 12 10 8 6 4

CONTENTS

LOG CABIN variation, mid-1800s
(Courtesy of Joan Kindler, Whitestone, New York)

INTRODUCTION

What may have seemed to be a never-ending voyage for the inhabitants of the Mayflower and other ships carrying people to the Americas was, in fact, the beginning of the arts known today as Americana.

In these pages, we will be dealing with one of the original art forms of Americana. Although quilt-making has been traced in history to the time of the ancient Egyptians, patchwork quilting began in America, with the Pilgrims.

Some quilters and critics have become bored with the traditional patchwork patterns. They feel that patchwork, like any other art form, must change with progress. They contend that the decor of today's homes does not lend itself to the "old-fashioned" designs; that many of these designs have worn themselves out of style. How wrong they are! The past provides a wealth of beautiful designs which should not be lost. Some of the most modern-looking patchwork was created in the nineteenth century. Given newly designed fabrics, a traditional patchwork pattern can be as lovely and challenging to create as a modern one.

For this book I have selected a group of patchwork patterns that were popular from the mid-nineteenth century until the early 1930s. I have chosen these patterns not only for their popularity among quilters in those years, but for their historic value and the unique stories behind their names and making. I hope these patterns will give quilters and critics another chance to understand how successfully they can be used in today's home.

It is well and good to go along with the times. It is sensible and indeed important to welcome change, if it is beneficial and can give us a more comfortable way of living. But it is equally important always to bear in mind that in blending in with the new, the old should not be forgotten or left to die.

CRAZY QUILT, 1886
(Courtesy of Joan Kindler, Whitestone, New York)

1.

TRADITIONS & HISTORY

Because their ships were small and cargo space limited, the only items the Pilgrims were able to bring with them to the New World were food, a minimum amount of durable clothes, and their quilts. The quilts served many purposes on board. They were used as dividers between families to give whatever privacy could be obtained in those close quarters. They were used as bedding, as protective covers for food and clothing, and as shawls on cold and wet days on the high seas. When the Pilgrims reached the shores of America, they were forced to continue living on their boats until homes could be built. The quilts took quite a lot of abuse over those years. Their endurance was far from exhausted, however, as they served for window covers, table cloths, and bedding in the new homes. They were mended and washed for many years to follow.

European quilts at that time were lovely creations. Their white tops and backs were held together with intricate and decorative white quilting stitches. Yet they were also sturdy and durable: they had to be to endure the years of wear the Pilgrims gave them.

It was through the years of mending these quilts with odd pieces of cloth that the quilts brought by the Pilgrims were christened with the first name in patchwork history. Because the quilts took on a deformed look, they were called "crazy quilts." There was no form and no beauty to these first crazy quilts. We cannot imagine how different they were from the cheerful crazy quilts we know today. And yet they provided the only bit of color to be found in the Pilgrims' homes.

After a time, when there was some semblance of normal life,. the women were once again able to quilt. Because of the scarcity of fabrics sent from England, the women were limited in the choice of fabrics they could use; they had to make do with what they had. With their keen eyes and practical sense, they devised colorful patterns, ingeniously using every scrap of fabric they could find. They pieced these scraps in blocks, set the blocks together, backed them—usually with flour or grain sacks— quilted them, and gave the resulting quilts titles that took their fancy. They named them after their colonies, their husbands' work, their dreams, their frustrations, their God, and stories from the Bible.

This, then, marked the beginning of the patchwork era. It is an era which has never ended.

Traditions go hand in hand with patchwork quilting. In many areas of the United States today, these traditions are still handed down from mother to daughter. They add spice and sensitivity to the art.

In the past, all girls were taught to make patchwork quilts at a tender age. They were given small swatches of fabric, usually cut from old clothes, to make squares composed of two patches. When they completed a number of these, they stitched them together, and then they were taught quilting stitches. By the age of ten, they were ready to make their first quilt. Making a quilt was keeping a young girl's mind innocent, protecting her from worldly temptations, from idle time and the devil's hand. Quilting was teaching a young girl to become an efficient woman; it was part of her upbringing as an ideal mate for marriage. But above all, making a quilt was a tradition that even the advent of commercially manufactured blankets did not change for many years.

Tradition obliged young girls to make twelve quilts before they could consider winning a husband. Then, when the young woman found her man, her engagement was announced by calling a quilting bee. Her relatives, neighbors, and close friends were invited to make the blocks for the quilt. Each block conformed to a motif selected by the girl's mother, and each block bore the name of its maker. With these blocks, a coverlet was then quilted by the bride-to-be. Upon completion, it became the thirteenth and the traditional "Album" quilt, so called because each contributor signed the patch she made. The Album quilt completed the bride's hope chest. Now she could make her marriage plans and begin to quilt coverlets for other people. As it turned out, it was usually her husband who received the four-teenth quilt!

Quilt-making has to be done when the hands of the quilter are warm and dry. It therefore took place in the evening when the outdoor chores were done and the dishes were dried and put away. It was done in the warmest part of the house, which usually was the kitchen area. The quilting room was always called "the Warm Room." If a visitor wanted the lady of the house in the evening hours, he would invariably find her in this room.

Traditionally, quilting was done on a quilting frame—a large wooden frame used to keep the quilt taut while sewing. These frames were cumbersome and space-consuming, so they were hung by ropes that ran through pulleys on the ceiling. When the quilt was not being worked on, the frame, with the quilt in it, could be pulled to the ceiling so it would be out of the way for the day's activities; in the evening, the frame was lowered to working level and balanced. This ingenious system allowed the frame to be angled by tying the ropes shorter in the back and longer in the front, providing greater accessibility to the area being quilted.

As communities began to grow, the quilting bee became increasingly popular. After church on Sundays, families would congregate, the men holding discussions and the women quilting. The quilting bees produced many lovely quilts which were sold at bazaars to raise money for the churches, and at political rallies to raise money for politicians. They were given to the minister's family and to newly arrived immigrants to the New World. Every quilt was made for a purpose and every quilt was used. Today, in contrast, it is easy to walk into a quilter's home and find quilts being stored in chests for posterity.

As the United States grew, many areas of the country became prominent for particular patchwork and quilting designs.

In New England the old-world quilting methods and designs were perpetuated. New England was too close to the mother land, England, to escape her influence. If the Yankee women did not quilt white-on-white quilts, they were making elegantly designed and embroidered crazy quilts of satin and velvets brought to port by traders from the Far East.

In the southeastern states, quilters gradually broke away from European quilting designs and the Album, or Friendship, quilts developed greatly. Because quilting bees continued to be very popular in this part of the country, it is very seldom that we can find quilts made by one individual.

WHITE ON WHITE, 1825
(Author's Collection)

ALBUM QUILT, 1850
Hudson Valley, New York
(Courtesy of Joan Kindler,
Whitestone, New York)

Detail of Album Quilt showing
signatures of quilters.

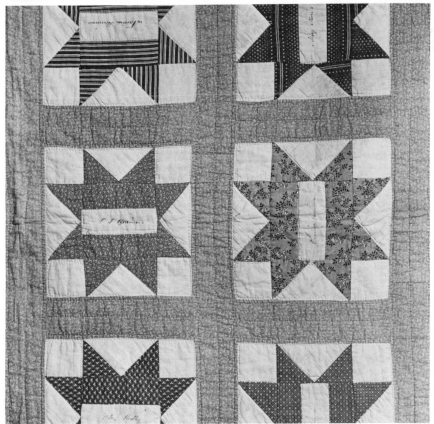

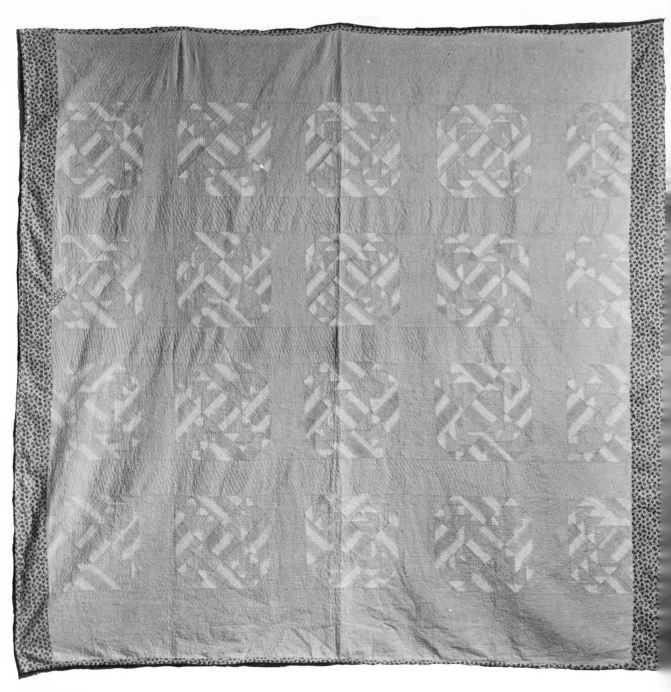

GOOSE IN THE POND, 1899
Dolan, South Dakota
(Author's Collection)

14

Southern women invented a very slow-paced and extremely beautiful method of quilting. Their appliquéd quilts were involved endeavors that required a great amount of skill to achieve perfection. Designs such as flowers and trees were cut out, then pieced and stitched on a block with a blind stitch.

The West produced a treasure of patchwork originality. It is in the West that the true American patchwork, as we know it today, originated. The pioneers' travels across the country represented some of the most romantic and adventurous history that we know. And the pioneer women, with their ginghams and calicoes, were not the least bit hesitant to reproduce their escapades in their quilt designs. Designs such as Flying Geese, Indian Hatchet, Bleeding Heart, and Wagon Wheel, as well as designs taken from Indian symbols, are typical examples of western patchwork.

Wherever they lived and whatever the distinctive designs they evolved, all American quilters had one thing in common. Through their determination to make it in a new land, with their fortitude and imagination, the women of the New World were able to translate their hopes, love, and fears into a beautiful craft. Through their ingenuity, they were able to create in their patchwork quilts durability and art. With the talents they possessed, they added color and warmth to their rustic homes. Above all, they showed that a woman's mind and talents were tools of creativity worthy of historic acclaim.

definitions of quilting terms

Appliqué. Designs, such as flowers, cut from pieces of fabric and laid on larger fabric blocks. The designs are then stitched to the block with a blind stitch.

Backing. The bottom layer of a quilt, consisting of a whole piece of fabric or seamed pieces. The fabrics generally used are muslins, solid-colored cottons, and simple prints.

Binding. The finishing of a quilt by covering its raw edges with the backing, which is brought over the pieced top, turned under, and stitched down. Strips of fabric cut on the bias or bias tape can also be used for binding a quilt. The strips are attached to the backing first, and then folded over the top and stitched down.

Block. An entire design made up of several shapes or unit pieces. It usually measures from 8 to 10 inches square; however, a block may be the size of a bed, so long as it constitutes one design.

Borders. Two- to four-inch strips of fabric that are used to separate blocks in a patchwork quilt for a decorative effect or to increase the size of the quilt. One or more borders can also be used around an entire quilt as a finish, and again to enlarge the quilt.

Coverlet. A quilted or tufted cover that is not used as a full bedspread. Coverlets are recommended to quilters because they best allow the true beauty of the designs to stand out.

Filler. Also referred to as the batt or batting, the filler is the middle layer of the quilt, placed between the patchwork top and the backing. It may be made from cotton, synthetics, down, or other materials. It provides warmth and gives body to the quilt.

Miter. To join together corners to form a right angle. Mitering is used to finish the corners of a binding or border.

Patchwork. The sewing together of small pieces of fabric to form geometric designs. The shapes most commonly found in patchwork are squares, triangles, diamonds, hexagons, and circles.

Piece. To sew together shapes or unit pieces so that they form a full design block.

Pieced Top. Completed designs of patchwork or appliqué sewn together to the dimensions of the quilt. The pieced top must be backed and quilted to complete the quilt.

Quilt. A cover, used as a bedspread or coverlet, consisting of three layers: the top is made of appliqué or patchwork; the middle layer is a filler or batt; and the bottom layer is a piece of muslin or cotton. The three layers are stitched together with a design, simple or elaborate, called quilting.

Quilting. A running stitch, gauged approximately nine stitches to an inch, which holds the three layers of a quilt together and also forms a decorative design.

Set. When all the blocks of a coverlet are complete, the act of coordinating the blocks by color and design and joining them to form a pieced top.

Stowing shapes. Refers to the separating or sorting of cut shapes or unit pieces by shape and color, and stringing them, like flowers on a lei, for future use.

Tufting. A method of holding the layers of a coverlet together by pulling through and knotting yarn or thread at spaced intervals.

Unit. The individual pieces or shapes of a pattern which make up a design block.

what is a quilt?

A coverlet becomes a quilt when it has been sewn together with quilting stitches—small running stitches that when used to hold the three layers of a quilted coverlet together form a design as well. A quilt can be made of two pieces of a solid-colored fabric, with a filler sandwiched between, which are then quilted with an intricate design. It can also consist of a patchwork top made of geometrical shapes that are sewn together to compose a design or series of designs, plus a backing and filler, held together with quilting stitches. An appliquéd top may be used instead of patchwork: here definite designs are cut and sewn to larger pieces of fabric. Again, a backing and a filler are used, and the three layers are quilted.

If a coverlet is not quilted, it is not considered to be a quilt: it is a patchwork coverlet or an appliquéd coverlet. The only exception is the crazy quilt. This is actually a patchwork coverlet that has been made of odd shapes of fabric which are held together with fancy embroidery stitches. It is backed, but no filler is used and it is not quilted. Because the stitchery makes the coverlet appear quilted, it has come to be called a quilt.

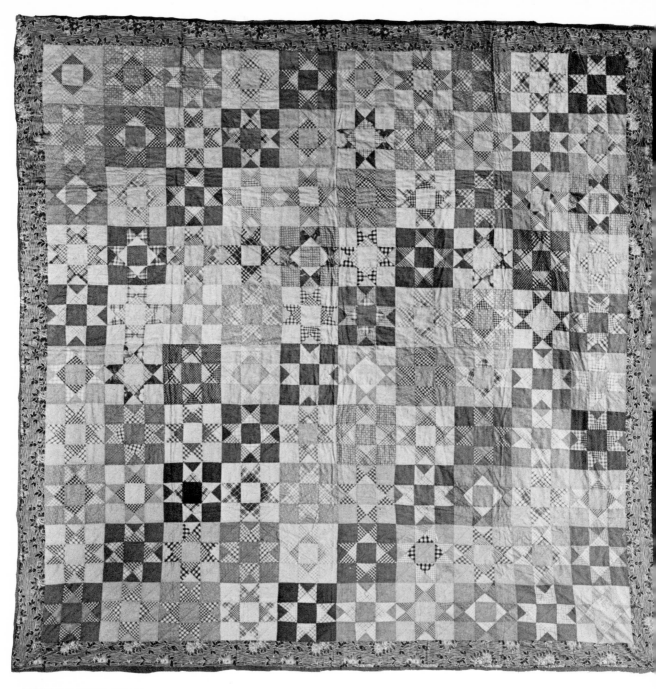

EIGHT POINT STAR, 1930
(Courtesy of Joan Kindler, Whitestone, New York)

2.

FABRIC & CUTTING

It takes very little special skill to become a quilt-maker. If you can thread a needle, you qualify. If you have fortitude, pride, and time, you will find that quilt-making will become a labor of love.

There are many methods of making quilts. But there are no set rules to follow. To thoroughly enjoy the work, you must choose a method that is easy and comfortable for *you*. When you make your first quilt, you will want quick methods because you will be anxious to see the final result. Although sewing by hand produces a finer product, and makes it possible to carry your work with you if you work by the block method, many quilters today use a sewing machine and are happy with the results. Experiment with a few pieces of fabric sewing by machine and by hand and then decide which is the most comfortable for you.

size & color selection

The first step in quilt-making is to determine the size of the quilt to be made. To do this, you must decide where and how the quilt will be used. Quilts can be made large enough to serve as full bedspreads, but in my opinion a quilt looks its best when it is made into a coverlet that covers just the top of a bed and is used with a solid-colored dust ruffle. This is the traditional way. A quilt can be a comforter, made primarily for warmth, as well. But why hide anything as lovely as a quilt under a bedspread?

Assuming that you will make a coverlet, plan for the bed sizes of today. The following can be used as a rough guide:

Twin	60" x 90"
Double	70" x 90"
Queen	80" x 110"
King	100" x 110"

On pages 50 through 78 you will find a selection of sixteen patterns. You may have to make adjustments in the size of your quilt or coverlet depending on the dimensions of blocks in these patterns. This is easily done. If a pattern gives a size of 60" x 90", it will fit a twin bed, but if you are making a coverlet for a queen-sized bed, you must add on blocks both across and down. If the blocks measure 10" square, you would add two blocks on the width and two blocks on the length. The resulting coverlet will be 80" x 110". A few extra inches will give your quilt a full and healthy effect. Always make your quilts a little larger rather than a little smaller than necessary: a skimpy-looking quilt will be a disappointment.

The next step is to select a color scheme. If you are not confident in your ideas about color, browse through fabric departments and remnant stores, and collect swatches. Or visit your local paint store and look at the color samples offered by paint manufacturers. They have excellent color wheels to guide you. Make a collection of these samples for future reference.

In choosing your colors, bear in mind that a finished quilt, with its allover design, offers a bold and colorful effect. If the colors in your room are soft and there is a lack of prints and patterns, your quilt color scheme can be bright and strong. If your room is full of bright colors and many prints and patterns, such as those on wallpaper and upholstery fabrics and drapes, then it would be sensible to limit your quilt to solid colors with occasional soft prints. Take your time in color selection; it is one of the most important preparations.

Select fabrics that sew together well. It will make piecing and quilting much easier. Your stitches will lie evenly and you will avoid puckering or bunched sewing lines. Cottons, linens, muslins, shirting fabrics, and blends containing cotton and polyester and the like go well together. Satins and silks make an elegant combination but are not appropriate for most patchwork quilts. But stay away from velvets as they do not quilt. (They make excellent embroidered or tied quilts, which you should not attempt making until you have become experienced in quilt-making or unless you are an expert seamstress.)

Look for fabrics that have small, dainty designs. The smaller the design, the prettier the quilt.

Be sure that all the fabrics you use are colorfast and pre-shrunk. There is nothing more disheartening than to have the colors run when you first wash your quilt. If you are uncertain whether a fabric is colorfast or preshrunk, make a simple test by washing measured samples of it in hot water to which a table-spoon of white vinegar has been added. With the fabrics of today, you should find everything in order.

If possible, always use new fabrics, and the best you can afford. If you use scraps left over from sewing or from old clothes, make sure they are clean and fresh before you begin sewing.

Once you have determined your colors and fabrics, it is time to choose a patchwork pattern. In Chapter 6 you will find sixteen traditional designs. It is amazing to discover that over a hundred years ago women created designs as daring and modern as any created today. The designs of the past offer a remarkable variety — what is reproduced here can give only a hint of the rich heritage upon which we can draw.

In the text that accompanies each design in this book, I offer suggestions on the type of decor I feel is best suited to the design. Make a careful decision in choosing your design, so that when your quilt is finished you will *use* it and not hide it away in a closet. Try to visualize the design as the allover pattern of the finished coverlet, in the room where you plan to use it. If when the top is pieced, you are not satisfied with it, you can modify the look by removing some blocks and using more solid-colored border, or by adding blocks to achieve a bolder effect.

yardage estimates

For the next step—estimating how much fabric you need—you will need patience, and a little courage! Glance through the patterns in this book and see how they are laid out and marked. This will help you to understand how to figure the yardage.

You now know the size and the colors. You have picked a pattern. First, calculate the amount of fabric needed for the backing. Simply multiply the length times the width of the quilt, adding the appropriate number of inches to length and width if you will use the backing as binding in finishing the quilt (see page 40).

To figure yardage for the pieced top, you need first to determine the measurements of the units in one block. For example, let us assume your pattern calls for ten-inch-square blocks.

On a piece of graph paper with five squares to an inch, scale out the block design, letting each square on the graph paper represent one inch (see the patterns in Chapter 6 as a guide). Then draw each unit in actual size. If you are using a design from this book, you do not need to do this, as the block designs and units are already laid out on graph paper and can be traced directly from the page.

Determine what color you will use for each unit. Then mark each unit in your scale design with its appropriate color. To help you, I have indicated whether a print or solid is needed and if it should be a light or a dark color.

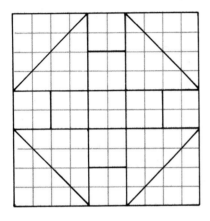

a.

b.

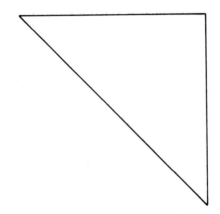

c.

First steps in calculating yardage:

a. Scale out block design to exact measurements on graph paper.

b. Draw each pattern piece in actual size.

c. Mark pattern units with appropriate color.

The design illustrated is Wrench.

Now tape together large sheets of tracing paper or use a roll of paper 36 inches wide (you must adjust accordingly if you use fabric of a different width). Draw each unit of the block that is to be a particular color *the number of times it is used in the quilt,* as illustrated. Draw the units close together, but draw them as they will be cut out—with the longest side of each shape aligned with the grain of the fabric—and *make sure you allow for a quarter-inch seam around each unit.* Draw or roughly indicate all the shapes of this color that you will need for the quilt. Then measure the amount of paper you have used, and round off upwards to the nearest quarter-yard. This is the amount of fabric you need for this color. Do this for each fabric to be used in the quilt. There

Calculate yardage needed for quilt by drawing each unit *by color and the number of times it is used* in actual size on paper that is 36″ wide. Remember to allow a quarter-inch for seaming, and add a quarter of a yard to the total for wastage and mistakes. The design illustrated is the Bowtie.

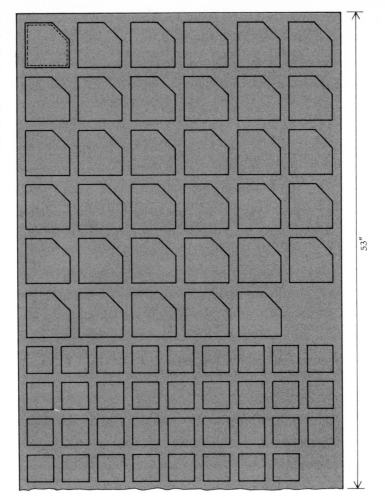

a. Buy 1¾ yards dark print fabric.

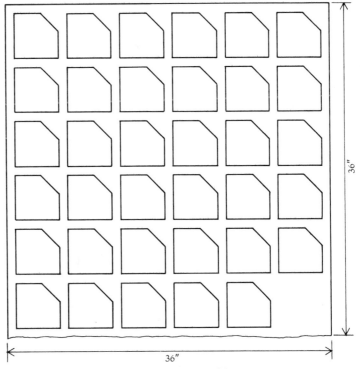

b. Buy 1¼ yards light print fabric.

are several other methods of calculating yardage, but I find that this one works best for me. Although it does require laying out every piece in the quilt top, this makes your calculations extremely accurate, and it gives you a useful guide for the actual cutting out of the pieces.

If you are using borders around the blocks, follow the same procedure as for the unit shapes in the blocks and calculate the additional yardage required for them.

Remember that there will be a certain amount of wastage, as the shape of the pieces may make it impossible for you to utilize every inch of fabric. However, save all scraps for future quilts.

Until you develop confidence in your estimates, always buy a little more fabric than you estimate you need. Again, leftover fabric can be used in future quilts.

cutting

Cutting your pattern and fabric constitutes the most important step in quilt making. When you cut, make sure that you are able to concentrate entirely on what you are doing. Plan to cut when you are sure that you will not be disturbed. Feeling relaxed and free from pressure assures precision cutting. Have on hand a sharpened hard lead pencil, a good, sharp scissors (preferably a dressmaker's scissors), and sheets of cardboard or fine sandpaper from which to make your patterns. I have found sandpaper to work the best because it holds the fabric when you cut. However, you should reserve one good sturdy pair of scissors for cutting sandpaper *only*; do not use your good dressmaker's scissors or any scissors you use for cutting fabric.

Trace each unit of the block, *plus a quarter inch for the seam allowance*, on the back of the sandpaper and cut out. You will use these shapes for all your cutting.

Press the fabric so that no wrinkles remain before laying the pattern shapes. Lay the fabric flat on a large, clean work surface, with the *right* side of the fabric up. Place the sandpaper shapes on the fabric (gritty side down), *making sure that the longer side of the shape is laid lengthwise on the fabric*, and draw around them. Draw as many outlines of each shape as you will need for the entire quilt. After all the drawing is done, check again to make sure that each shape is laid in the same direction.

Each shape must be cut individually. This method guarantees precision piecing. As you cut, stow the shapes by color and design on a doubled sewing thread.

batting & backing

Certain batts or fillers for quilting are better than others. The new polyester and Dacron batts on the market are recommended for their strength and durability. After many washings, these batts retain their body and they do not mat or bunch up as do many of the cotton batts. The synthetic batts give quilts a puffy effect, which many experienced quilters think is undesirable, yet this effect can make a quilt look full and alive. I suggest that beginners use these batts. They are easy to work with in the quilting process, and when the quilt is finished the puffiness will cover any mistakes in the quilting stitch that you may have overlooked.

Cotton batts are difficult to work with. They tear easily because they are loosely felted. They do not retain their body when they are washed and they mat terribly. Many companies are now using a glaze finish on all batts, including the cotton batts. This finish does add some body to the cotton batts, but not enough to alleviate the problems they present in washing.

Many quilters use old blankets as batts. They serve the purpose well, but they are hard to quilt and their weight when wet causes the quilting stitches to break easily in washing. Broken stitches must be repaired after each washing, making the care of your quilt more difficult.

Down and kapok are also used as filling, particularly when warmth is desired. They are not recommended for the quilting process, but they work well in a coverlet that will be tufted or tied.

Muslin, monk's cloth, India cloth, and cotton are excellent fabrics to use for backings. They are inexpensive and they quilt well. Textile manufacturers are making printed muslins that can add an exciting look to the quilt. Using a printed fabric as a backing allows the quilt to become reversible. Sheets also make a good backing. If you use cotton sheets, however, wash them first, as the cotton may not be fully preshrunk.

DOUBLE WEDDING RING, 1944
(Courtesy of Joan Kindler, Whitestone, New York)

3.

PIECING THE QUILT TOP

piecing by hand

In preparation for piecing a patchwork top by hand, you need a good thread, a number 10 needle, a ruler or stitch gauge, and a thimble.

Always use new thread, as an old spool may be warped or weak. Pick an all-purpose thread for piecing. (The new polyester threads work well, but I prefer cotton.) The length of the needle you select is up to you. A short needle works best because it is easier to maneuver, but it does take time to learn to handle it. Be patient—with practice you will develop the facility you need. A ruler or seam gauge is important both in piecing and quilting. Measuring your stitch as you go along will help you to make even seams and perfect corners. A comfortable, snugly fitting metal thimble is essential. When your thimble is too loose, you cannot get a good leverage on the needle to make straight, even stitches.

Before you begin piecing, lay out one block, as you would a jigsaw puzzle. Doing this with the unsewn pieces gives you an understanding of how the units should be pieced. During your piecing, always keep a finished block nearby for reference.

Knot your thread (it should not be more than 20" long) and, using a small, straight running stitch, begin sewing the units together *on the wrong side of the fabric*. The running stitch is the main stitch involved in quilt-making. It is used for the piecing and quilting process, as well as for attaching borders and bindings.

The running stitch is worked from right to left. Bring the needle in and out of the material, gauging the stitches at nine per inch. Space them evenly, checking to see that the tension of the stitch is the same on both sides of the fabric. Do not take more than three stitches at one time. Doing so will throw off your stitch gauge.

Care should be taken in starting and finishing off with the thread. A tight knot should be made in the thread before starting each new seam.

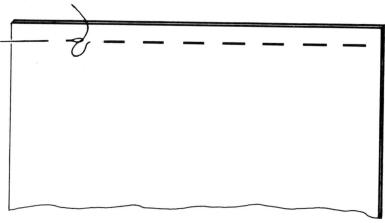

Simple running stitch: this is the stitch used most in quilt-making.

Back-stitch four stitches at the beginning and end of each seam. The back stitch is used to reinforce the seam: bring the needle up through the material and take a small stitch back, inserting the needle where the last forward stitch was started. Bring the needle out slightly in front of the forward stitch. Then take another forward stitch and repeat the process once again.

Be sure that your seam is as close to a quarter-inch as possible.

It is usually best to start piecing with the center units, as this makes accurate joining easier. After each block is pieced, press the seams to one side. Do not open seams. Complete one block at a time.

If you are working by the block method, you will quilt each block separately before setting the blocks together, as described in Chapter 5. If you are quilting with a frame, the entire top is set before quilting.

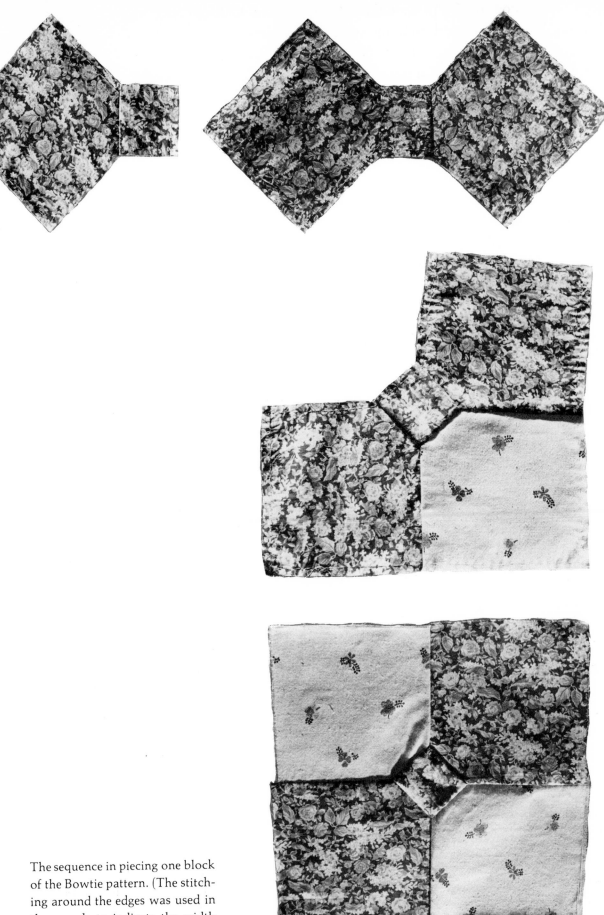

The sequence in piecing one block of the Bowtie pattern. (The stitching around the edges was used in the sample to indicate the width of the seams.)

The blocks are laid out on a large work surface in the order that they will be sewn. If there are different multicolored blocks, distribute them by color or value and not by print (unless the pattern specifies otherwise). When you are satisfied with the composition of the blocks, begin setting them with a quarter-inch running-stitch seam. Join the blocks row by row. Give special attention to the corners where more than two pieces meet, so a perfect joining can be made. If you are using borders between each block, attach them as you set the blocks.

Borders are used between blocks to separate the designs and, in many cases, to enlarge the size of the quilt.

The sequence in piecing one blo of the Rob Peter to Pay Paul p tern. Piecing curves like these difficult to do accurately. Ke your seams an even quarter-in slashing each curve as it is do and check as you go along make sure the pieces align w each other. (Sequence by Mau Greenbaum)

The width of the borders depends on personal preference, but standards widths are either two or four inches. The way of attaching the borders will vary with the design and the quilting method you use, but two simple ways are shown here.

If the quilt is to be quilted by the frame method, attach one top (horizontal) border to each block, as shown in the illustration. then sew together vertical strips of these blocks until you reach the length of the quilt. The side (vertical) borders are the same width as the top borders, but as long as the quilt. Assemble strips of blocks and border strips alternately, as shown. (Remember that you will need an extra border at the bottom of the last row of blocks, as indicated by the shaded area in the illustration.)

If you are quilting by the block method, add a top and a side border to each block as shown in the illustration, working from left to right and from top to bottom. (Remember that the last blocks on the right and the bottom will need extra borders to complete the design, as shown by the shaded areas in the drawing.)

Attaching a single border to a quilt.
 a. Borders attached for assembling when working by the frame method.
 b. Assembling the blocks. Shading indicates extra pieces to complete design.
 c. Borders attached for assembling when working by the block method.
 d. Assembling the blocks. Shading indicates extra pieces to complete design.

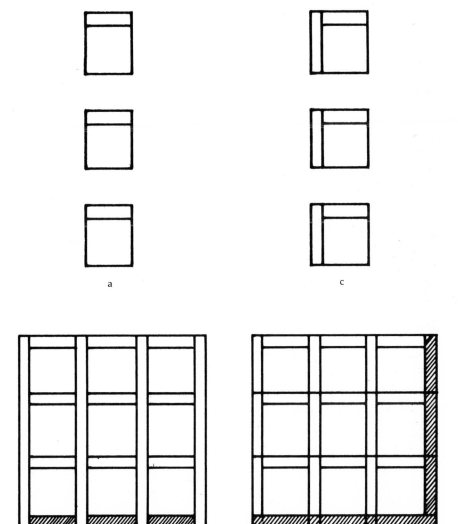

a

c

b

d

Adding a border around the entire quilt is a nice finishing touch; several borders can add a dazzling effect to a quilt design. Borders can be used to add or mute color or to increase the size of a quilt after you have finished piecing it. The width of the outside border depends, again, on personal preference. Four-inch borders are the standard; however, many quilters use a series of borders in different widths on one quilt. The outside borders are made with four single strips of fabric: the top and bottom borders are the exact width of the top; the side borders are the length of the quilt plus the width of the borders. The outside borders are, of course, attached after the pieced top is completed.

If you are quilting by the block method (see page 42), you will join the three layers of the quilt together in each block *before* setting the blocks together. If you quilt by the traditional method — on a frame — you are now ready to piece the top. Sew the blocks together with running stitch — remember to sew on the *wrong* side of the blocks. Set the blocks in rows, and then sew the rows together in the same way.

When you have set all the blocks and borders, press the finished top on the wrong side of the fabric with a steam iron. Begin at the center and press to the outside edges. All the seams should be perfectly straight and there should be no puckering in the fabric. The top is now ready to be quilted as described in Chapter 5.

piecing by machine

If you prefer, you can piece and set your quilt top by machine. In my view, however, the only real advantage of machine piecing is that it is faster. Everything else remains the same. You must take care in cutting and piecing. A machine will not hide mistakes. And if you work by machine, you cannot carry your work around with you.

Set up the machine in a well-lighted area and on a large, sturdy work surface. Keep the iron plugged in, as there is much more pressing involved in machine piecing then in hand piecing. Set the tension regulator at normal and the stitch regulator at 2 gauge or 20 stitches per inch. If your machine is equipped with a seam guide, set it at a quarter-inch. Check your bobbin to make sure there is enough thread and, as in hand sewing, use a good thread. In piecing, make sure that you have experimented previously with the placement of the units in the block and keep a finished block nearby for reference. Remember to sew on the wrong side of the units. Back-stitch at the end of every seam. After every four or five units are pieced, press the seams to one side. Check all meeting points to make sure that they meet precisely.

If your design contains curves, I do not recommend that you sew the curves by machine, unless you are extremely familiar with machine sewing. If you do sew the curves by machine, be sure to slit each seam after sewing so that it lies properly. Iron each curve as it is sewn. The importance of pressing in machine sewing cannot be stressed enough. Iron frequently in order to ensure a well-made machine-sewn top.

Baste the blocks well before setting by machine. Again, press the blocks as you go along and check for mismatched seams and puckering. Set in rows and press with a steam iron, as in hand piecing, when the top is finished.

...ocks such as these, both vari-
...ions of Rob Peter To Pay Paul,
...ould not be pieced by machine.
...nly by hand sewing can you
...hieve really smooth curves.
...locks by Mauve Greenbaum)

BASKET QUILT, 1930
(Courtesy of Joan Kindler, Whitestone, New York)

4.

QUILTING

When the quilt top is pieced and set, it is time to join the three layers of your quilt together. There are two ways of doing this: quilting and tufting.

There are three methods of quilting for you to choose from: quilting with a frame, quilting by block, and quilting by machine. Quilting with a frame is the traditional way, and some people feel that if you have not had the experience of quilting on a frame, you are missing the romance of the art. But if you quilt by frame, you need a large work area, and every time you need that area to do other work, the frame must be stored.

Quilting by block is a fine modern method which eliminates the need for a quilting frame. Quilting by block is the method I favor because it makes quilting a portable needlecraft: you complete small sections of your quilt at a time, and you can take your work with you everywhere you go.

Quilting by machine is time-saving, but the work done by machine cannot compare to that of the hand. The method of quilting you choose is up to you, and you should pick whatever is most convenient and comfortable.

quilting with a frame

Department stores and craft shops sell quilting frames at moderate prices. These frames are a bargain if you live in a small house or apartment because they fold up for storage easily. The manufacturers supply directions for installing the quilt in the frame.

You can also make your own frame, but I do not recommend this unless you have room that you can dedicate solely to quiltmaking. In order to store the home-made frame, you must disassemble it. When you are ready to resume work, you will find that it is difficult to replace the quilt in the frame with the same tension it had when first put in, and a different tension will cause an uneven quilting stitch. Nevertheless, many people find making a frame a satisfying experience, and I provide instructions in case you want to try it.

You need two pieces of 1″ x 2″ lumber cut the length of the pieced top plus twelve inches at each end. Two more 1″ x 2″ strips of wood must be cut the width of the top plus 12 inches at each end. Put the strips of wood together with C-clamps, the longer pieces crossing over the shorter ones, as shown in the illustration. Now wrap the frame with strips of cloth or muslin. Use double thickness for wrapping and wrap the cloth securely. Hold the wrapping in place with a few thumbtacks. Now the frame is ready to be used. Place it over the backs of four high-backed chairs. (Old wooden chairs with knobs on each corner are the best to use.) The ideal room to work in is large and well lighted, a room that you will enjoy working in. Pleasant and relaxing surroundings are important if you are to enjoy making a quilt.

Prepare the quilt backing. It must be the size of the pieced top (including the border, if any), plus four inches on all sides.

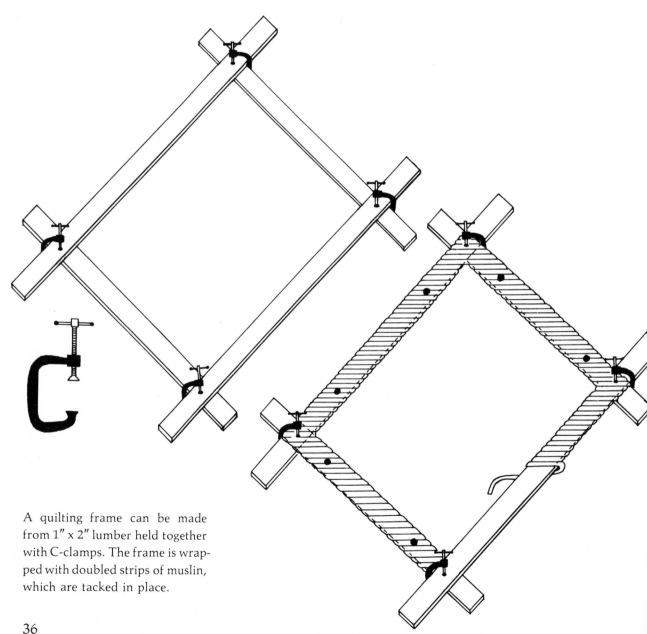

A quilting frame can be made from 1″ x 2″ lumber held together with C-clamps. The frame is wrapped with doubled strips of muslin, which are tacked in place.

You will probably have to seam lengths of fabric together for the backing. Be sure to press the seams well.

With the wrong side of the fabric up—facing the ceiling—baste one long side of the backing to the wrapping on one long side of the frame. Use a firm basting stitch. Then sew the other side of the backing to the opposite side of the frame. Loosen the C-clamps and stretch the back tightly by moving the side of the frame towards you. Do one side at a time. If possible, get someone to help you. When the backing is taut, secure the clamps well.

Unroll as much batting as you need and carefully place it over the backing. You will have to stretch it, as it is compressed when first unrolled. Be gentle when stretching it so that you will not make holes that cannot be repaired. Start in the middle of the batting and pull very carefully to the edges. The batting should be a little smaller than the pieced top. Spread it evenly and thinly—a thin batt is easier to quilt.

Lay the pieced quilt top next. Center it properly and measure from the edges of the quilt top to the edges of the basted backing to make sure it is centered.

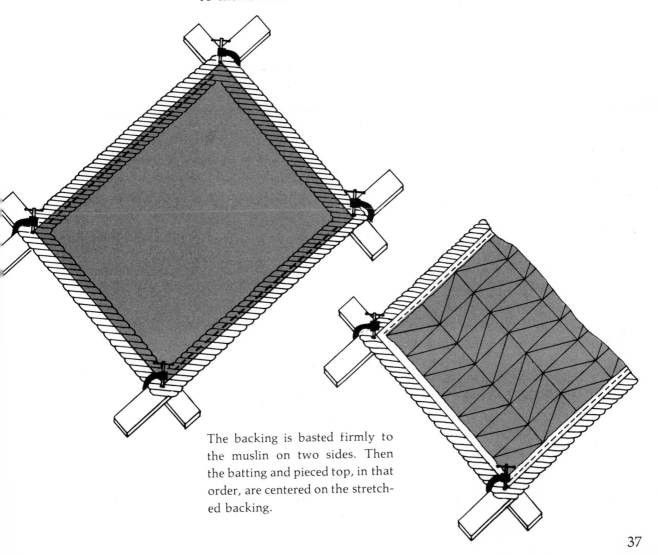

The backing is basted firmly to the muslin on two sides. Then the batting and pieced top, in that order, are centered on the stretched backing.

37

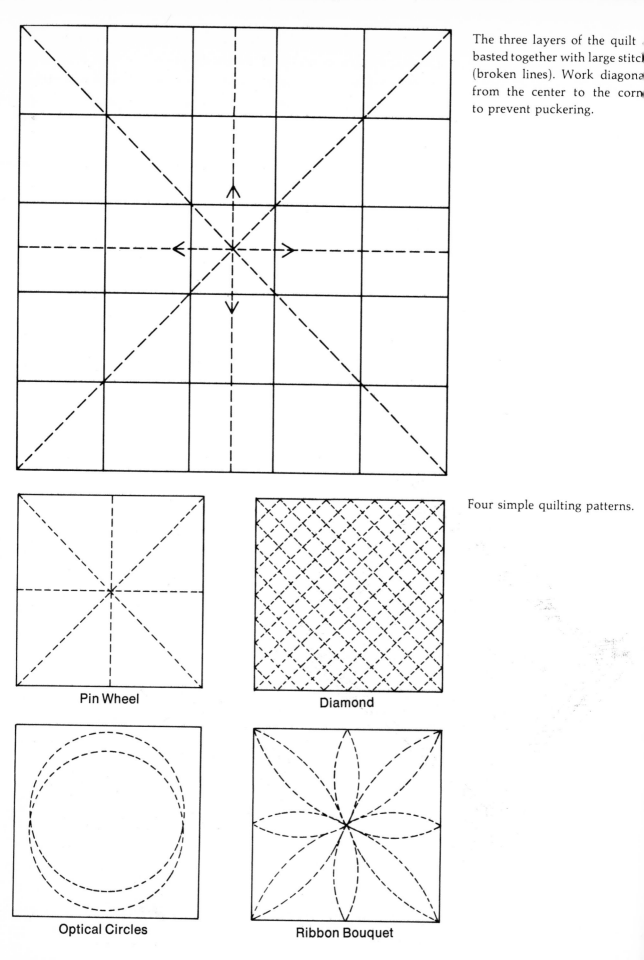

The three layers of the quilt basted together with large stitch (broken lines). Work diagona from the center to the corn to prevent puckering.

Four simple quilting patterns.

Pin Wheel

Diamond

Optical Circles

Ribbon Bouquet

Baste all three layers together with large stitches. Do this on a diagonal, beginning in the center and working to the corners. If the quilt seems to be sagging, loosen the clamps again and restretch.

There are many quilting patterns from which to choose. Unless you are skilled in the art of quilting, the simple patterns are best for you. The most basic one, a very beautiful design, consists of outlining the seam line of each unit in the block. This is done by using a running stitch as close to the seam as possible. If you decide to use a more elaborate design for your quilting, select one that works *with* the pieced top; don't use a design that detracts from the beauty of the piecing.

You can create your own designs by using compasses and rulers or the plastic templates used by decorators and architects to draw your original version onto the fabric, or you can draw freehand if you are so inclined. Use a hard lead pencil because this erases easily. Quilting patterns are also available in department stores and craft shops. These patterns are perforated, and are transferred to the fabric by applying a powder over the perforations.

Mark whatever pattern you choose on the quilt top. Start at the center and continue to a half-inch in from the edges.

A number 10 needle is the one most commonly used in quilting. It may be uncomfortable to work with in the beginning. As you use it, you will notice that it will begin to curve. When it does, you will have an ideal quilting needle. If a number 10 needle is too small for you to work with, a number 9 sharp can be used. It is longer and has a larger eye.

Many fabric stores and notions counters now carry special quilting thread. Because this thread is waxed, it can only be used for hand quilting. Polyester thread can also be used for quilting; it works exceptionally well on synthetic fabrics. Usually white thread is used in quilting. Colors have been introduced recently, but colored thread requires a skillful hand, as mistakes show up easily. Unless you have quilted before, do not use colored thread.

Perfect quilting consists of nine stitches to the inch. Gauge yourself by this and you will achieve perfection. Working from the center to the ends of the quilt, use a small, straight, even running stitch. When the running stitch is used for quilting, the needle must penetrate the work at a right angle. This position is necessary so that enough of the batting and backing is picked up to bind all three layers together. The stitch on the back must be the same length as the stitch on the top. Knot your thread and start from the backing side. Give the thread a sharp pull so the

titch gauge: nine stitches to the ,ch, actual size.

knot will come through the backing and lodge in the batting, where it cannot be seen. Quilt to a half-inch in from the edges of the quilt. Back-stitch at the end of each quilting row. When you run out of thread, and when you finish, make the knots on the backing. Keep them as small as possible and snip loose threads as close to the knot as you can.

The running stitch as used in quilting: the two-step operation is necessary in order to penetrate the three layers of the quilt.

After a quilt is quilted, it is then removed from the frame and the process of binding or finishing the quilt begins. This can be done in two ways.

The backing, if enough fabric is allowed, can be used for the binding. Bring it over the quilt top, fold under, and blind-stitch into place.

If you prefer, you can choose the fabric that is most pleasing from the quilt and cut on the bias in strips. Piece the strips to make two strips measuring the length of the quilt and two measuring the width of the quilt. The width of the strips depends on how much of it you want to show: usually two-inch strips suffice. Sew the strips to the backing first, and cut the corners on an angle for mitering. Bring the binding over the quilt top, fold under, and hem, using a blind stitch.

The steps in mitering a corner.

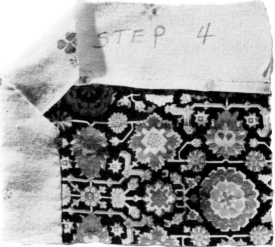

Begin at the right side of the work, catch the folded edge of the binding to the pieced top with the needle and thread. Space stitches evenly.

Finally, miter all corners.

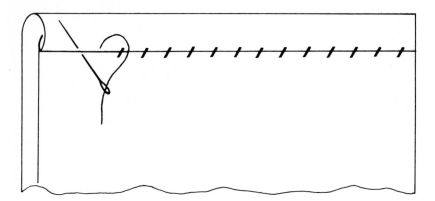

A hem stitch is used to finish the edges of the quilt.

quilting by block

Block quilting seems to me the best quilting method for today because it allows you to take your work with you anywhere. You need no frame. You piece and quilt a section at a time. After all the blocks are pieced and quilted, they are set together and finished.

Piece one block at a time. If you are using borders, piece the top border and one side border at the same time. Next, cut a piece of batting a half-inch smaller than the block (plus borders), and a piece of the backing fabric a half-inch larger than the block (plus borders). Baste the three layers together. Draw your quilting design on the block. In quilting, you can use a small board as a surface to work on, or you can use your lap. Starting at the center of the block, quilt to a half-inch in from the edges. Continue piecing and quilting the blocks until you have completed the number needed for the quilt.

To set the blocks, lay two of them face to face and pull the backing and batting back. Use a small and neat running stitch to join the pieces. Open the blocks and lay face down. Overlap the backing of one block on the second one. Fold the fabric under and hem with a blind stitch.

To make a nice reversible quilt, you might decorate the hem lines by folding both backings in a half-inch, butting them, and using a whip stitch to attach them. Take seam binding or a decorative trim such as rickrack and blind-stitch it over the seams.

Finish the quilt by binding as described in the section on quilting by frame.

To attach two blocks in block quilting, place them face to face, pull back backing and batting, and stitch the block tops together with running stitch. (In the sample, the tops are a dark solid.)

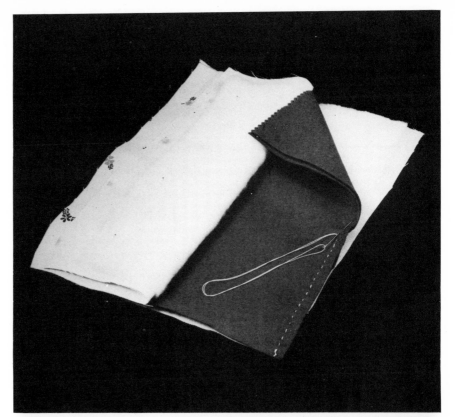

To attach the backings, fold under the edge of one block and overlap the raw edge of the other block. Then blind-stitch the blocks together.

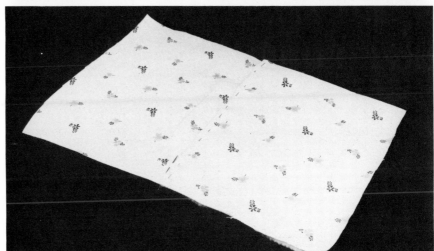

For a reversible quilt, decorate the seam lines of the backing by attaching a trim.

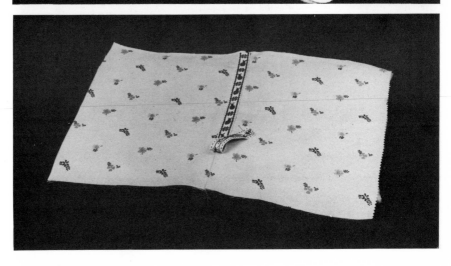

(Samples made by Mauve Greenbaum)

quilting by machine

Any type of sewing machine can be used for quilting. Set the machine at ten stitches per inch. It is essential to use a quilting foot with a rounded front: it will work with a lighter tension and keep the fabric from puckering and the batting from bunching. This type of foot has a built-in guide, which should be set at two inches. The stitching must be done carefully and the design must be followed accurately, as you cannot rip stitches once you have started to sew.

Lay the three layers of the quilt on a large work surface, or the floor. Baste the layers securely, being careful not to move the quilt until it is completely and firmly basted. A diamond pattern is the best design to quilt by machine. Use a yardstick and a hard lead pencil to draw the design. Draw diagonal lines from corner to corner to form an X. At two-inch intervals from the X lines, draw parallel diagonal lines, until the entire quilt has been patterned into diamond shapes.

Make sure that there is enough surface space to maneuver the quilt while you are sewing.

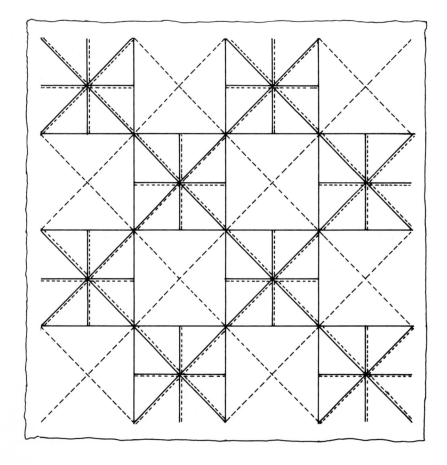

A large diamond quilting pattern drawn on the pieced top. Quilting is also to be done along the seam lines of the patchwork blocks. The quilting-stitch pattern complements the design of the patchwork blocks.

Starting with the first X, sew the two lines in opposite directions. Then sew all the lines parallel to one side of the X, in the same direction as the line of the X. Turn the quilt and sew the remaining lines in the opposite direction. Quilt to within a half-inch of the edges.

You can also quilt the outline of the design by machine. Begin at one corner of the quilt and sew as close to the seam lines as possible. Do not clip threads as you go. Instead, release the pressure foot, pull a few inches of thread at the end of the seam, and continue on to the next seam. Clip threads and tie knots at the finish.

If the backing of the quilt is to be used in finishing, fold it over the quilt top. Fold the binding under and stitch by machine or by hand. To machine-stitch the binding, you must sew through the three layers of the quilt. Keep the stitch as close to the edge as possible. Bring the binding over the quilt top, fold and hem by using a zig-zag stitch on the machine or blind-stitch by hand. In all finishing, be sure to miter the corners.

Machine sewing is not recommended for the fancier quilting designs. There are companies who will do this work. Check the list of suppliers at the end of this book for names of these companies.

The sequence of machine stitching: sew along the heavy lines in the direction of the arrows; then sew along all the light solid lines, and, finally, along all the broken lines.

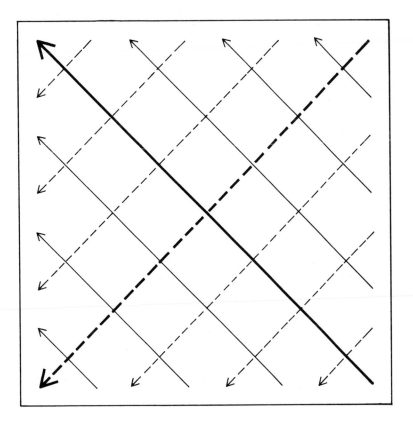

Tufting a coverlet is a simple procedure. Mark the points at which tufting is to be done; then pull thread or yarn through and tie in double knots. (Sample by Mauve Greenbaum)

5.

TUFTING & TYING

Tufting is a method of holding the three layers of a coverlet together by pulling through and knotting yarn, thread, or string at spaced intervals. No sewing is needed in this method. It is most effective in comforters, and can create as lovely an effect as quilting.

You can use any type of batting in tufting. If quilt batting is used, lay the three layers of the coverlet on the floor and baste well. If the coverlet is to be used as a comforter, down or kapok makes an excellent filler. In using these fillers, you must first attach the pieced top to the backing. Sew them together on the wrong sides, leaving a twelve-inch opening on the last corner. Through this opening, pull the coverlet through to the right side. Then stuff the down or kapok through the opening and sew it closed with a whip stitch. Lay the filled coverlet on the floor and knead the filler into place until it is evenly distributed. Baste the three layers well to keep the filler in place until tufting is completed.

Using a pencil or chalk, mark at intervals where the tufting will be done. With down or kapok, the tufting should be done at two-inch intervals; with cotton or polyester batting, the tufting does not have to be so close.

The thread should be colorful and strong. Embroidery thread, yarn, or string can be used; test it first to make sure that it will tie well and hold a knot.

Use a needlepoint or embroidery needle to draw the thread through. Working from the top of the coverlet, put the needle through the three layers and bring back through the top. Leaving two inches of thread at each end, cut and tie an ordinary double knot. Continue until the entire coverlet is tufted.

When the tufting is completed, finish the coverlet with binding as usual.

6.

16 TRADITIONAL PATCHWORK QUILT PATTERNS

In this chapter you will find a collection of patchwork patterns based on the design of the quilts in the accompanying photographs. Because modern beds are quite different in size from beds of the nineteenth and early twentieth centuries, the sizes specified in the patterns are different from those of the photographed quilts. (The sizes given include the borders between blocks.) The photographs are intended only to illustrate design and color.

In some of the patterns I suggest that borders should be used. This is optional, since many of these designs look just as lovely without the borders. As with so many aspects of quilt-making, it is a matter of personal preference. It is a good idea, however, to baste borders between a few blocks to see if this achieves the effect you are looking for. Remember, too, if you decide to use borders, that you must add the yardage you will need to your calculations. Measurements given include borders between blocks but not outside borders, unless a border for finishing is specified.

I recommend cottons and blends, such as cotton with a percentage of polyester or Dacron, for most of the patterns given here; exceptions are noted in the accompanying text.

Note: The patterns that follow are reproduced on graph paper with five squares to the inch. The blocks are drawn at the scale of one square = one inch; the unit shapes are drawn actual size. To help you lay the pieces out for cutting correctly, arrows indicate the direction of the grain of the fabric. Remember to allow a quarter-inch around each shape for seams!

PRESENTATION QUILT, 1890
Bennington, Vermont
Author's Collection

IRISH CHAIN QUILT, 1871
Westminster, Maryland
Made by Angeline Baublits

49

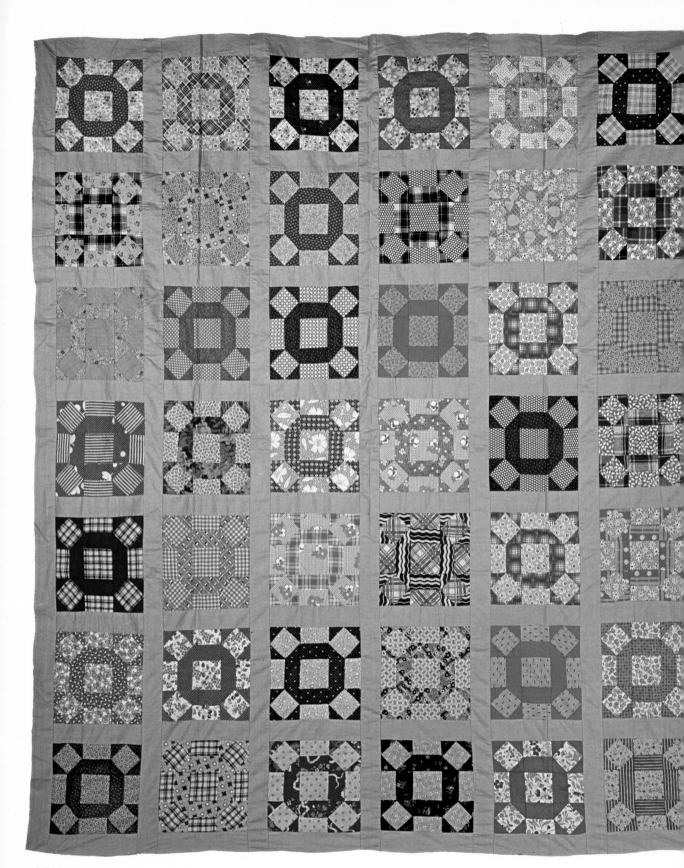

ROLLING STONE QUILT, 1875
Salt Lake City, Utah
Author's Collection

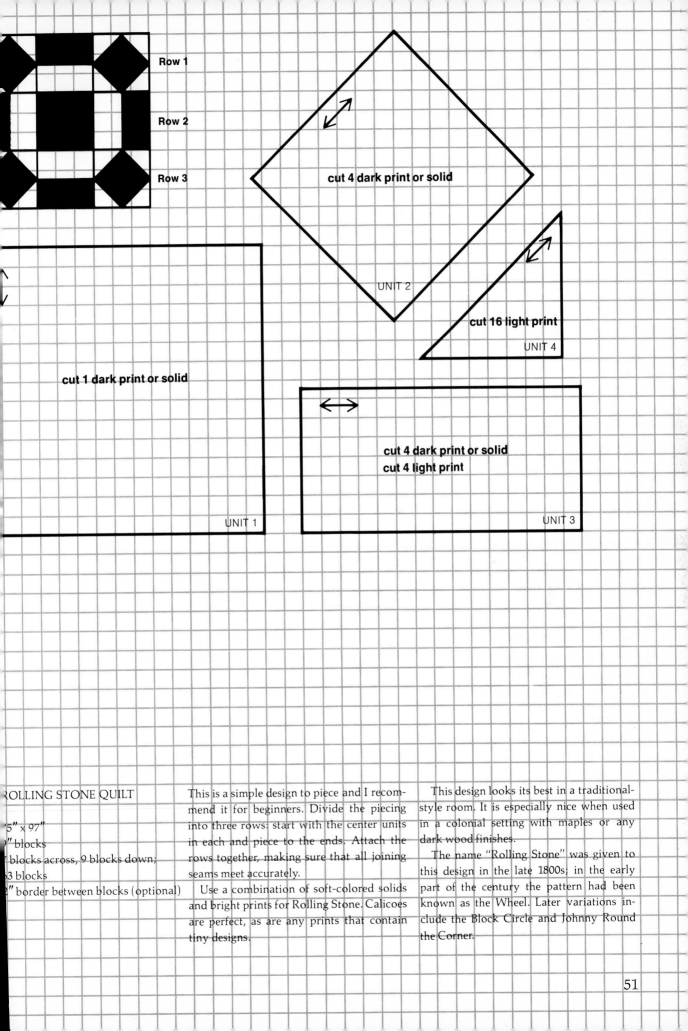

Row 1

Row 2

Row 3

cut 4 dark print or solid

UNIT 2

cut 16 light print

UNIT 4

cut 1 dark print or solid

cut 4 dark print or solid
cut 4 light print

UNIT 1

UNIT 3

ROLLING STONE QUILT

5" x 97"

" blocks

blocks across, 9 blocks down;
3 blocks

" border between blocks (optional)

This is a simple design to piece and I recommend it for beginners. Divide the piecing into three rows: start with the center units in each and piece to the ends. Attach the rows together, making sure that all joining seams meet accurately.

Use a combination of soft-colored solids and bright prints for Rolling Stone. Calicoes are perfect, as are any prints that contain tiny designs.

This design looks its best in a traditional-style room. It is especially nice when used in a colonial setting with maples or any dark wood finishes.

The name "Rolling Stone" was given to this design in the late 1800s; in the early part of the century the pattern had been known as the Wheel. Later variations include the Block Circle and Johnny Round the Corner.

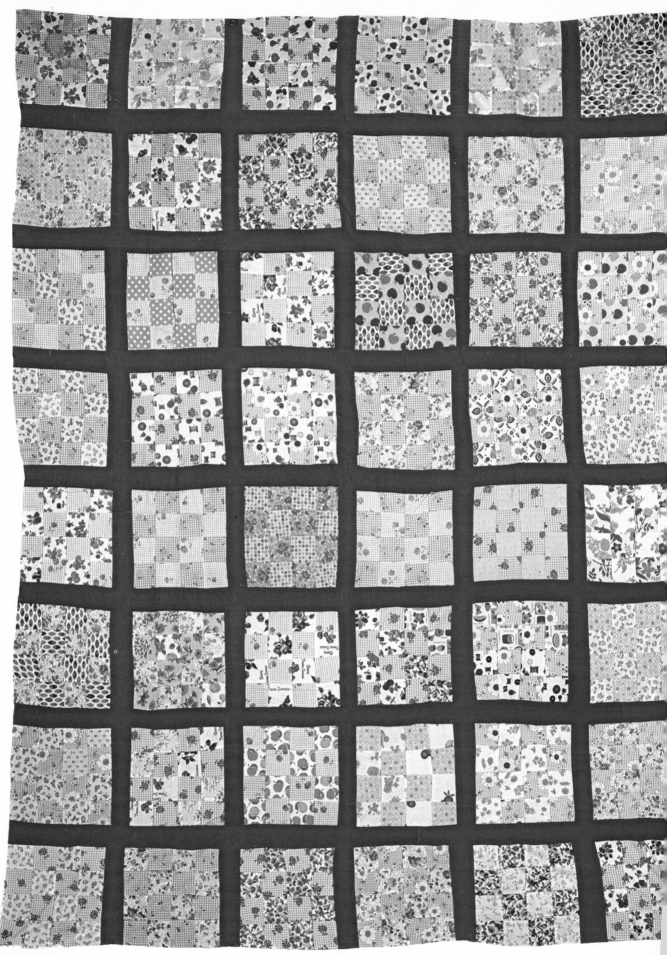

16 PATCH QUILT, 1930   Preston Hollow, New York   Courtesy of Mamie Ga

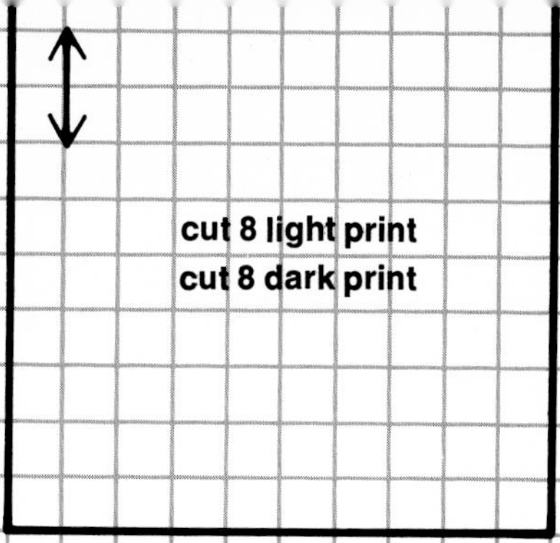

cut 8 light print
cut 8 dark print

QUILT

oss, 8 blocks down;

tween blocks

This is an excellent design for machine piec-ing. It can be tufted and tied rather than quilted, and I recommend it for beginners. The square units are set alternating one light and one dark throughout the block. If you use odd scraps of fabric for the squares, arrange them in the blocks by color and not by print.

The 16 Patch should be made of very colorful fabrics. It is an excellent design for using up scraps left over from other quilts. Cottons and blends are best to use if you are quilting, but wools, velvets, and satins can be used if you are tufting. (B that when you use fabrics suc and satin, you must have the c cleaned.)

The 16 Patch looks good in a decor. It can be made for any si it is particularly suitable for a as it is a cheerful design and doesn't show dirt.

16 Patch was given its name i It is a variation of the tradition so named because each square ca into four square patches of the sa

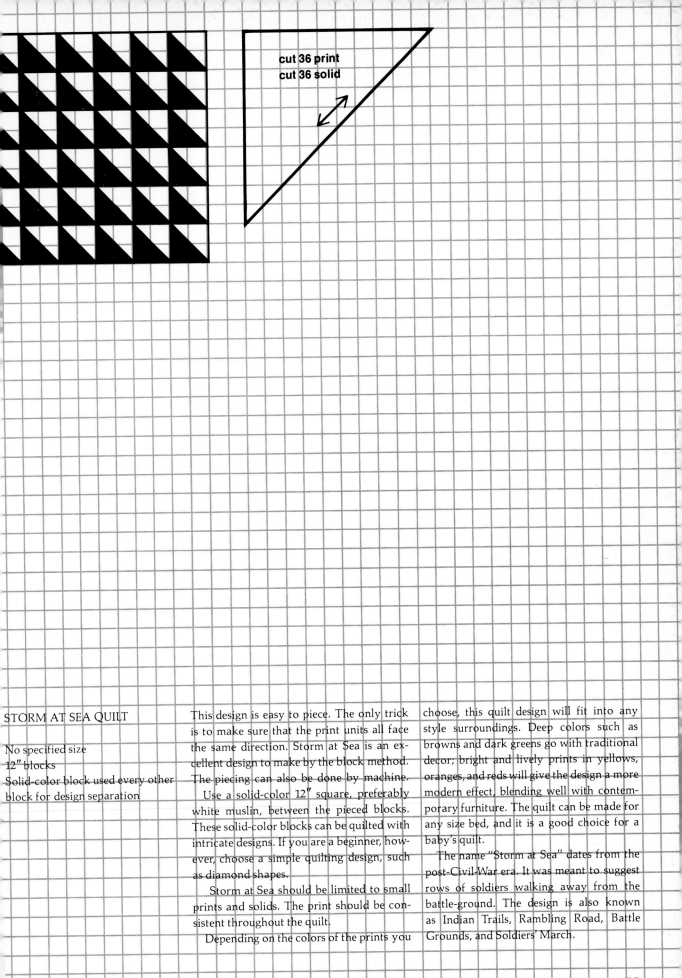

cut 36 print
cut 36 solid

STORM AT SEA QUILT

No specified size
12" blocks
Solid-color block used every other block for design separation

This design is easy to piece. The only trick is to make sure that the print units all face the same direction. Storm at Sea is an excellent design to make by the block method. The piecing can also be done by machine.

Use a solid-color 12" square, preferably white muslin, between the pieced blocks. These solid-color blocks can be quilted with intricate designs. If you are a beginner, however, choose a simple quilting design, such as diamond shapes.

Storm at Sea should be limited to small prints and solids. The print should be consistent throughout the quilt.

Depending on the colors of the prints you choose, this quilt design will fit into any style surroundings. Deep colors such as browns and dark greens go with traditional decor; bright and lively prints in yellows, oranges, and reds will give the design a more modern effect, blending well with contemporary furniture. The quilt can be made for any size bed, and it is a good choice for a baby's quilt.

The name "Storm at Sea" dates from the post-Civil-War era. It was meant to suggest rows of soldiers walking away from the battle-ground. The design is also known as Indian Trails, Rambling Road, Battle Grounds, and Soldiers' March.

IRISH CHAIN QUILT, 1920
Manchester, Maryland
Made by Sarah J. Hann

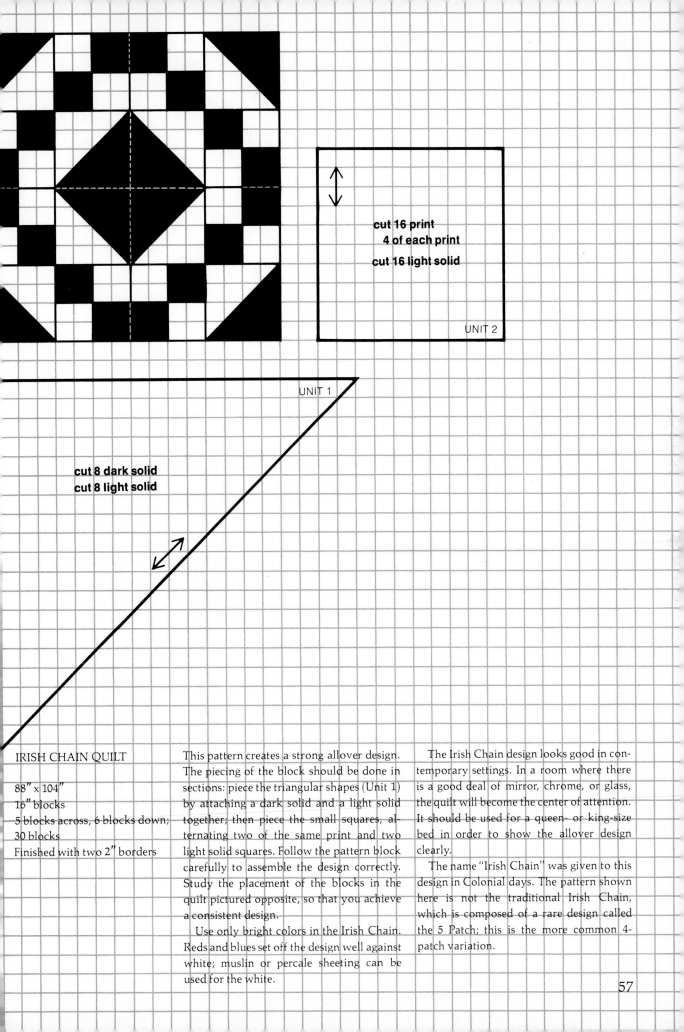

cut 16 print
4 of each print
cut 16 light solid

UNIT 2

UNIT 1

cut 8 dark solid
cut 8 light solid

IRISH CHAIN QUILT

88" x 104"
16" blocks
5 blocks across, 6 blocks down;
30 blocks
Finished with two 2" borders

This pattern creates a strong allover design. The piecing of the block should be done in sections: piece the triangular shapes (Unit 1) by attaching a dark solid and a light solid together; then piece the small squares, alternating two of the same print and two light solid squares. Follow the pattern block carefully to assemble the design correctly. Study the placement of the blocks in the quilt pictured opposite, so that you achieve a consistent design.

Use only bright colors in the Irish Chain. Reds and blues set off the design well against white; muslin or percale sheeting can be used for the white.

The Irish Chain design looks good in contemporary settings. In a room where there is a good deal of mirror, chrome, or glass, the quilt will become the center of attention. It should be used for a queen- or king-size bed in order to show the allover design clearly.

The name "Irish Chain" was given to this design in Colonial days. The pattern shown here is not the traditional Irish Chain, which is composed of a rare design called the 5 Patch; this is the more common 4-patch variation.

WRENCH QUILT, 1925
Bennington, Vermont
Author's Collection

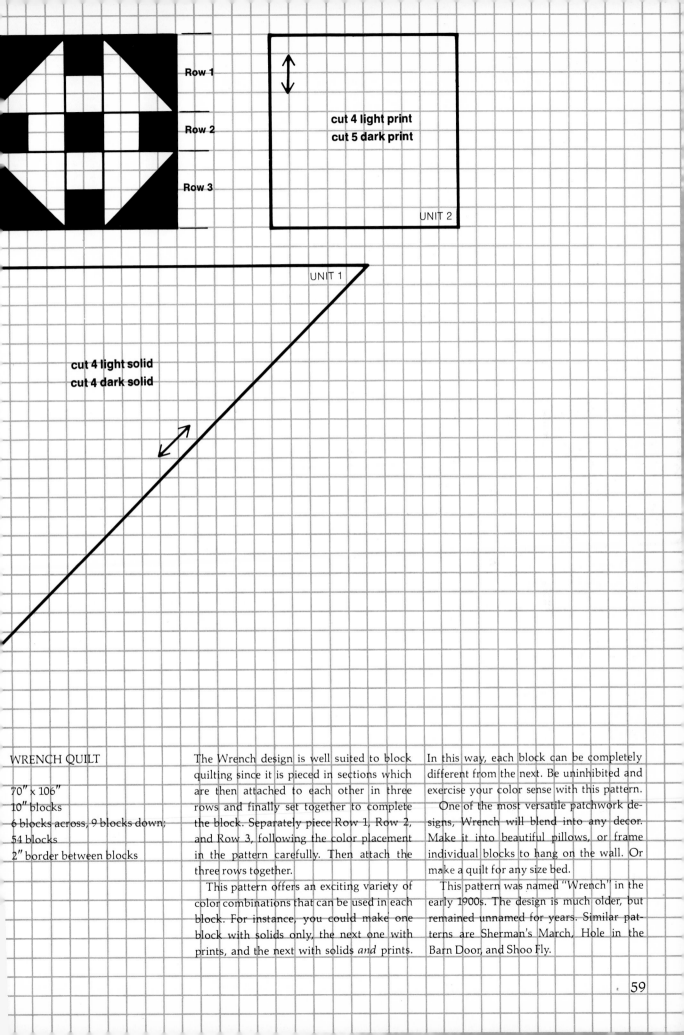

Row 1

Row 2

Row 3

cut 4 light print
cut 5 dark print

UNIT 2

UNIT 1

cut 4 light solid
cut 4 dark solid

WRENCH QUILT

70" x 106"
10" blocks
6 blocks across, 9 blocks down;
54 blocks
2" border between blocks

The Wrench design is well suited to block quilting since it is pieced in sections which are then attached to each other in three rows and finally set together to complete the block. Separately piece Row 1, Row 2, and Row 3, following the color placement in the pattern carefully. Then attach the three rows together.

This pattern offers an exciting variety of color combinations that can be used in each block. For instance, you could make one block with solids only, the next one with prints, and the next with solids *and* prints.

In this way, each block can be completely different from the next. Be uninhibited and exercise your color sense with this pattern.

One of the most versatile patchwork designs, Wrench will blend into any decor. Make it into beautiful pillows, or frame individual blocks to hang on the wall. Or make a quilt for any size bed.

This pattern was named "Wrench" in the early 1900s. The design is much older, but remained unnamed for years. Similar patterns are Sherman's March, Hole in the Barn Door, and Shoo Fly.

BASKET OF SCRAPS QUILT, 1930
Manchester, Maryland
Made by Sarah J. Hann

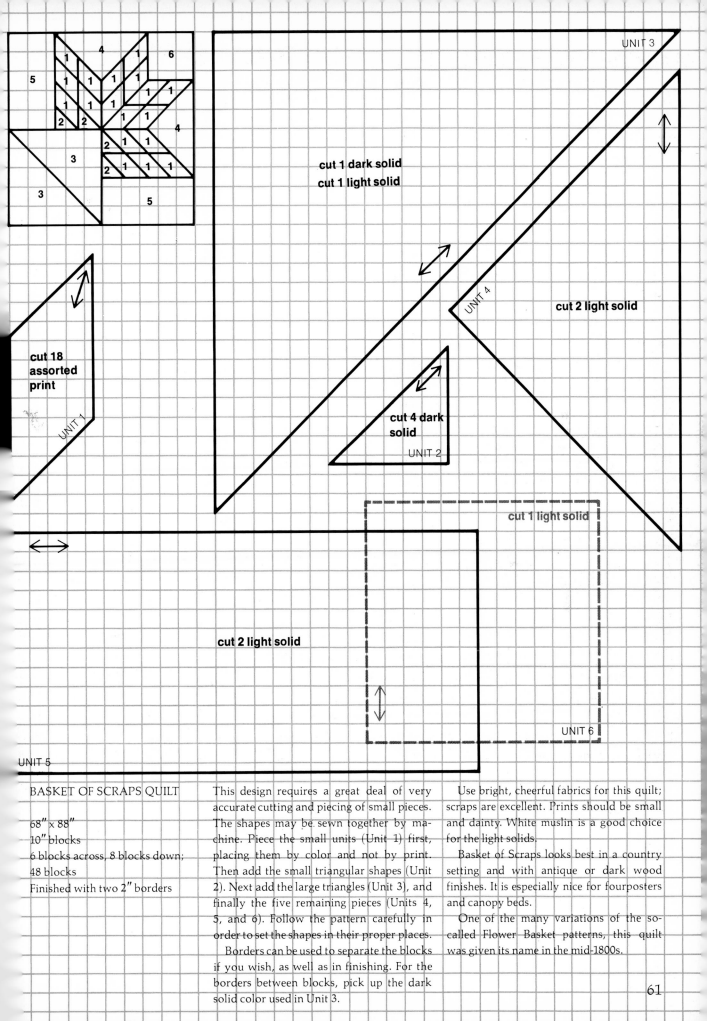

cut 1 dark solid
cut 1 light solid

UNIT 3

UNIT 4

cut 2 light solid

cut 4 dark solid

UNIT 2

cut 18 assorted print

UNIT 1

cut 1 light solid

cut 2 light solid

UNIT 6

UNIT 5

BASKET OF SCRAPS QUILT

68" x 88"
10" blocks
6 blocks across, 8 blocks down;
48 blocks
Finished with two 2" borders

This design requires a great deal of very accurate cutting and piecing of small pieces. The shapes may be sewn together by machine. Piece the small units (Unit 1) first, placing them by color and not by print. Then add the small triangular shapes (Unit 2). Next add the large triangles (Unit 3), and finally the five remaining pieces (Units 4, 5, and 6). Follow the pattern carefully in order to set the shapes in their proper places.

Borders can be used to separate the blocks if you wish, as well as in finishing. For the borders between blocks, pick up the dark solid color used in Unit 3.

Use bright, cheerful fabrics for this quilt; scraps are excellent. Prints should be small and dainty. White muslin is a good choice for the light solids.

Basket of Scraps looks best in a country setting and with antique or dark wood finishes. It is especially nice for fourposters and canopy beds.

One of the many variations of the so-called Flower Basket patterns, this quilt was given its name in the mid-1800s.

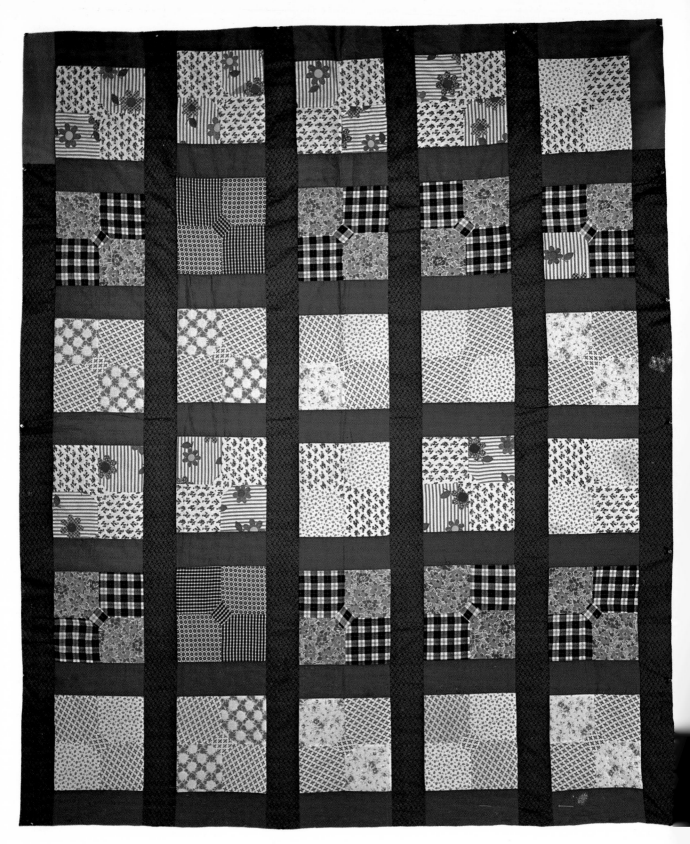

BOWTIE QUILT, recent
Preston Hollow, New York
Author's Collection

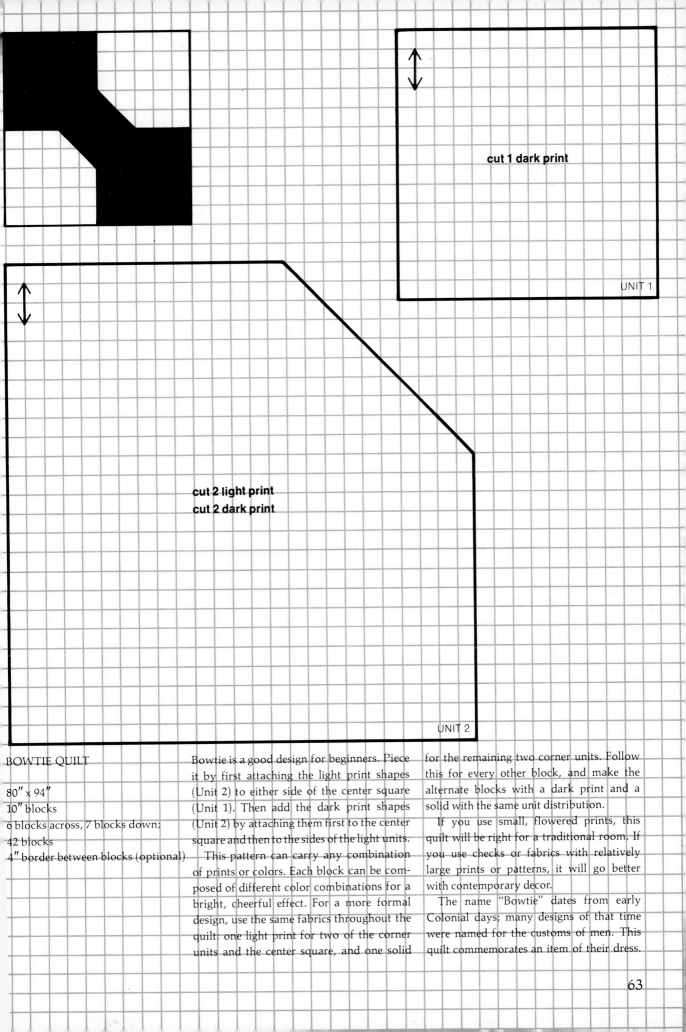

cut 1 dark print

UNIT 1

cut 2 light print
cut 2 dark print

UNIT 2

BOWTIE QUILT

80" x 94"
10" blocks
6 blocks across, 7 blocks down;
42 blocks
4" border between blocks (optional)

Bowtie is a good design for beginners. Piece it by first attaching the light print shapes (Unit 2) to either side of the center square (Unit 1). Then add the dark print shapes (Unit 2) by attaching them first to the center square and then to the sides of the light units.

This pattern can carry any combination of prints or colors. Each block can be composed of different color combinations for a bright, cheerful effect. For a more formal design, use the same fabrics throughout the quilt: one light print for two of the corner units and the center square, and one solid for the remaining two corner units. Follow this for every other block, and make the alternate blocks with a dark print and a solid with the same unit distribution.

If you use small, flowered prints, this quilt will be right for a traditional room. If you use checks or fabrics with relatively large prints or patterns, it will go better with contemporary decor.

The name "Bowtie" dates from early Colonial days; many designs of that time were named for the customs of men. This quilt commemorates an item of their dress.

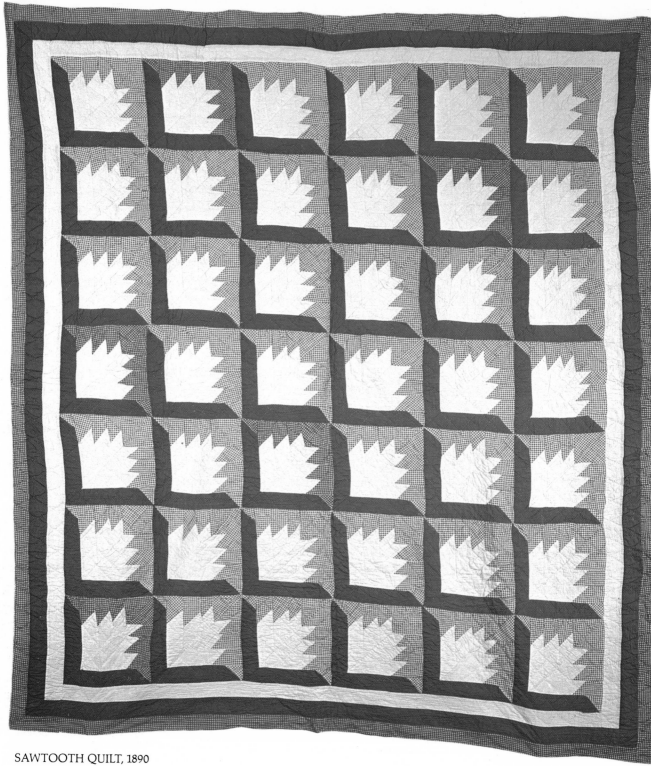

SAWTOOTH QUILT, 1890
Manchester, Maryland
Made by Sarah J. Hann

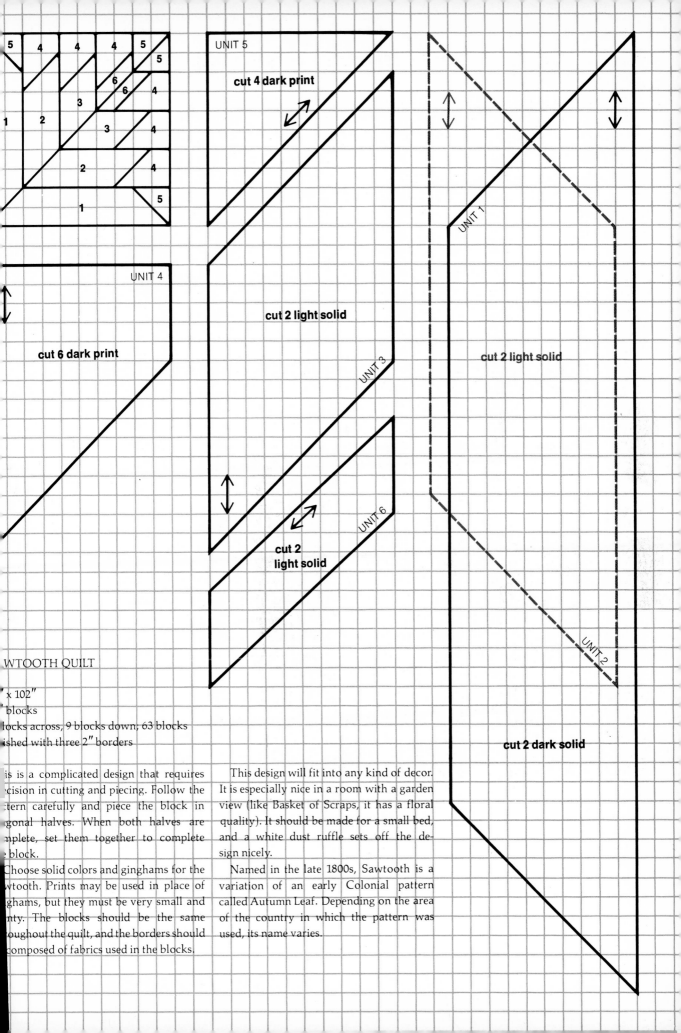

UNIT 5

cut 4 dark print

UNIT 4

cut 6 dark print

cut 2 light solid

UNIT 3

UNIT 6

**cut 2
light solid**

UNIT 1

cut 2 light solid

UNIT 2

cut 2 dark solid

5 4 4 4 5 5 6 6 4 3 3 4 1 2 3 4 2 4 1 5

WTOOTH QUILT

" x 102"
" blocks
locks across, 9 blocks down; 63 blocks
ished with three 2" borders

is is a complicated design that requires
cision in cutting and piecing. Follow the
tern carefully and piece the block in
gonal halves. When both halves are
mplete, set them together to complete
block.
Choose solid colors and ginghams for the
wtooth. Prints may be used in place of
ghams, but they must be very small and
nty. The blocks should be the same
roughout the quilt, and the borders should
composed of fabrics used in the blocks.

This design will fit into any kind of decor.
It is especially nice in a room with a garden
view (like Basket of Scraps, it has a floral
quality). It should be made for a small bed,
and a white dust ruffle sets off the design nicely.
Named in the late 1800s, Sawtooth is a
variation of an early Colonial pattern
called Autumn Leaf. Depending on the area
of the country in which the pattern was
used, its name varies.

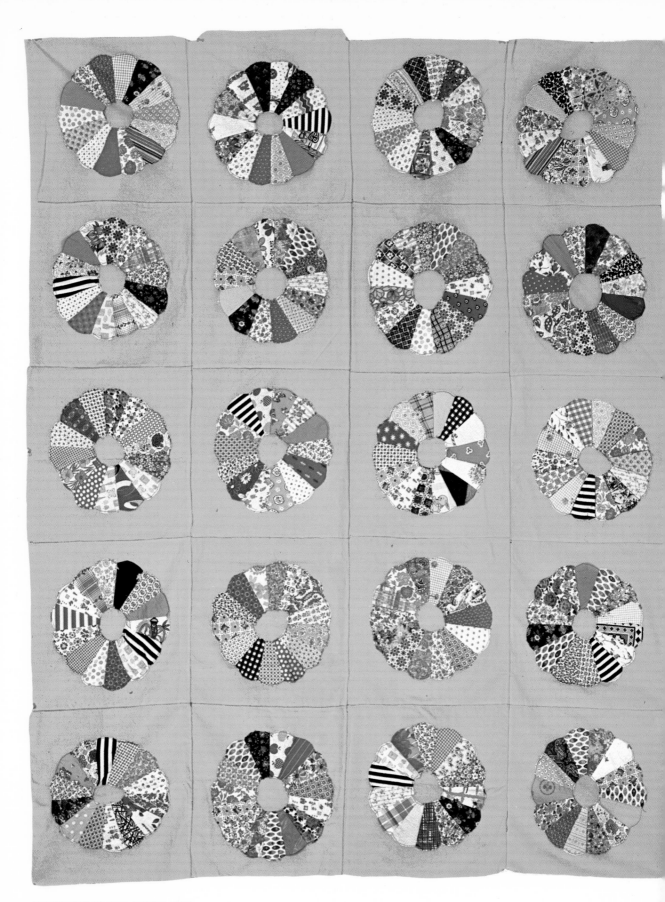

DRESDEN PLATE QUILT, 1930
Preston Hollow, New York
Made by Mamie Galt

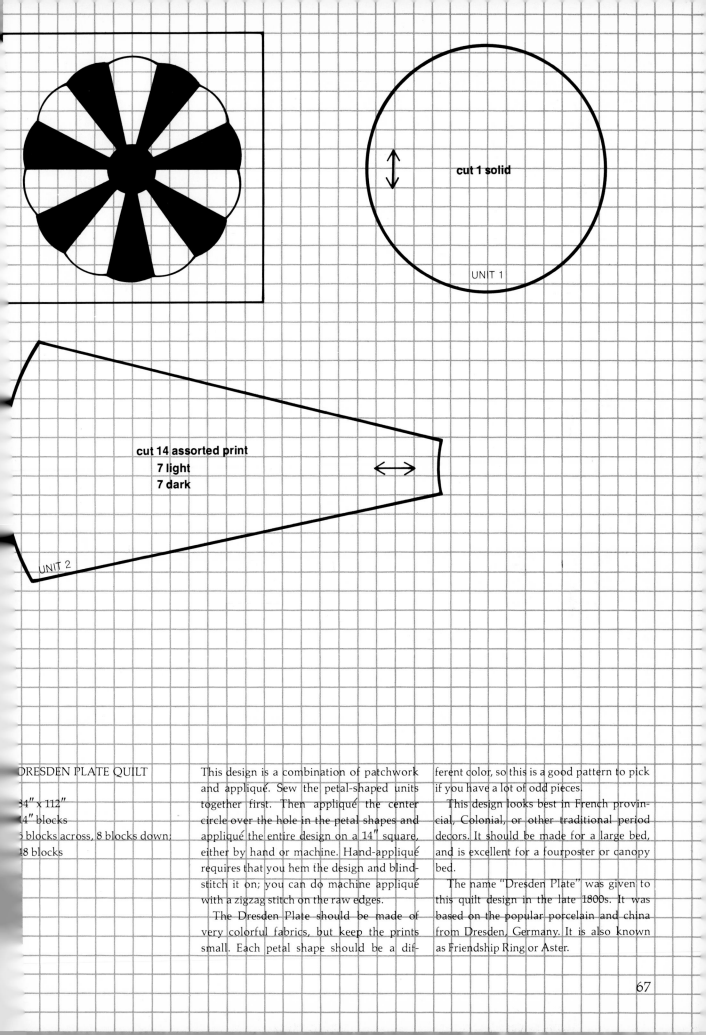

cut 1 solid

UNIT 1

cut 14 assorted print
7 light
7 dark

UNIT 2

DRESDEN PLATE QUILT

84" x 112"
14" blocks
5 blocks across, 8 blocks down;
18 blocks

This design is a combination of patchwork and appliqué. Sew the petal-shaped units together first. Then appliqué the center circle over the hole in the petal shapes and appliqué the entire design on a 14" square, either by hand or machine. Hand-appliqué requires that you hem the design and blind-stitch it on; you can do machine appliqué with a zigzag stitch on the raw edges.

The Dresden Plate should be made of very colorful fabrics, but keep the prints small. Each petal shape should be a dif-ferent color, so this is a good pattern to pick if you have a lot of odd pieces.

This design looks best in French provincial, Colonial, or other traditional period decors. It should be made for a large bed, and is excellent for a fourposter or canopy bed.

The name "Dresden Plate" was given to this quilt design in the late 1800s. It was based on the popular porcelain and china from Dresden, Germany. It is also known as Friendship Ring or Aster.

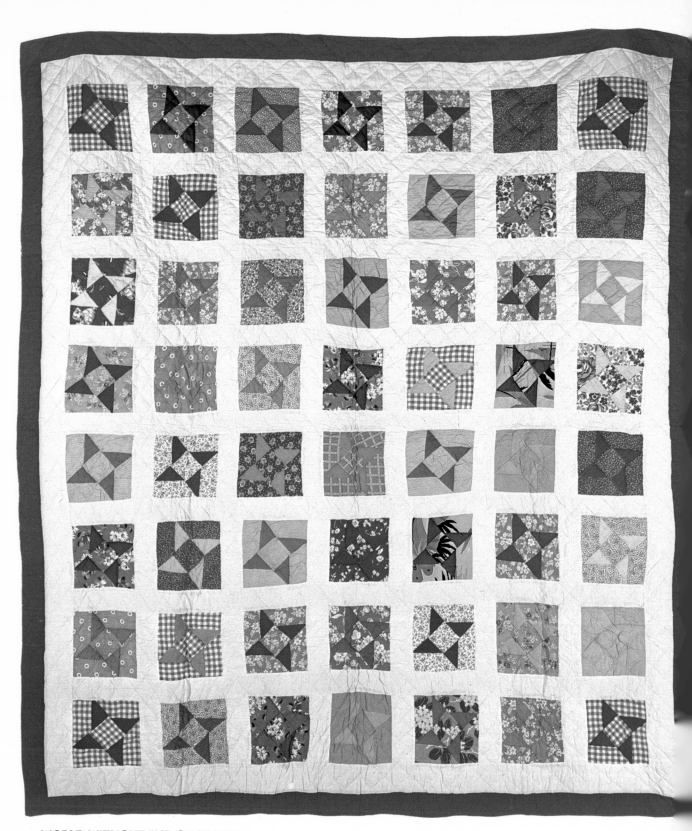

WORLD WITHOUT END QUILT, 1880
Charleston, South Carolina
Author's Collection

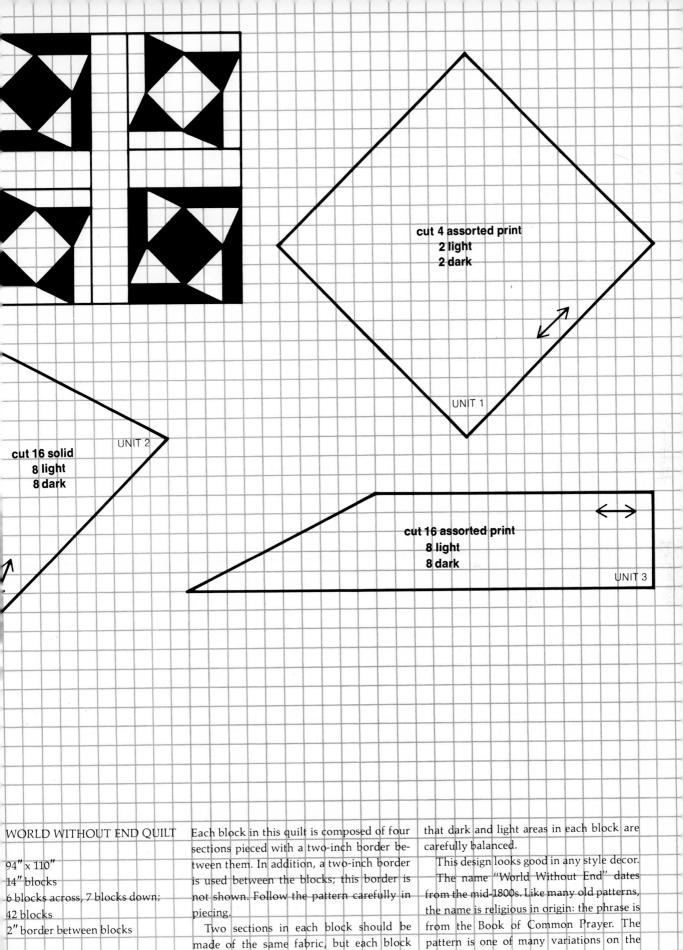

cut 4 assorted print
2 light
2 dark

UNIT 1

cut 16 solid
8 light
8 dark

UNIT 2

cut 16 assorted print
8 light
8 dark

UNIT 3

WORLD WITHOUT END QUILT

94" x 110"
14" blocks
6 blocks across, 7 blocks down;
42 blocks
2" border between blocks

Each block in this quilt is composed of four sections pieced with a two-inch border between them. In addition, a two-inch border is used between the blocks; this border is not shown. Follow the pattern carefully in piecing.

Two sections in each block should be made of the same fabric, but each block can be made of different sets of fabric. Note that dark and light areas in each block are carefully balanced.

This design looks good in any style decor.

The name "World Without End" dates from the mid-1800s. Like many old patterns, the name is religious in origin: the phrase is from the Book of Common Prayer. The pattern is one of many variations on the Pinwheel design.

GRANDMOTHER'S DREAM QUILT, 1895
Cheyenne, Wyoming
Author's Collection

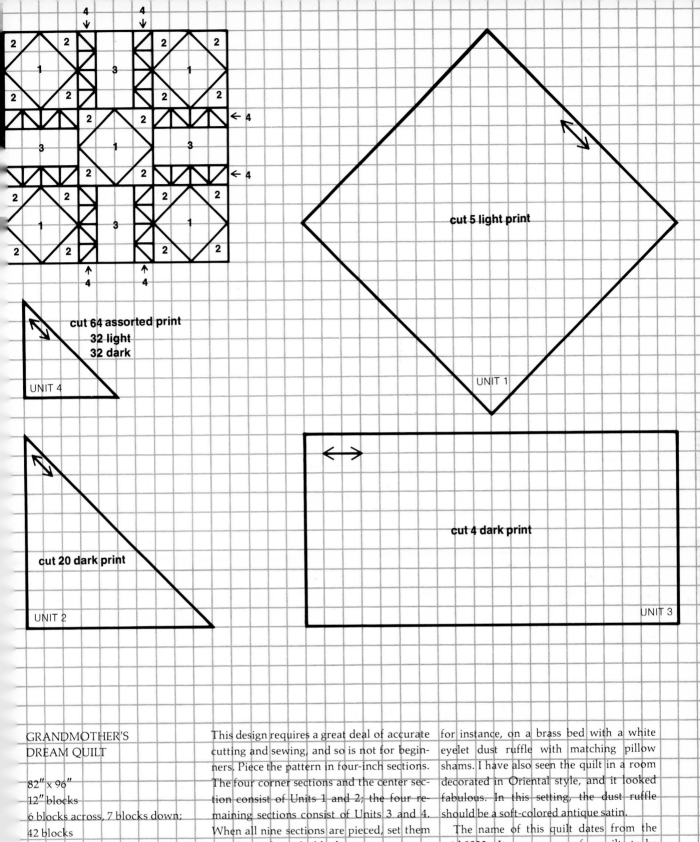

cut 64 assorted print
32 light
32 dark

UNIT 4

cut 5 light print

UNIT 1

cut 20 dark print

UNIT 2

cut 4 dark print

UNIT 3

GRANDMOTHER'S DREAM QUILT

82″ x 96″
12″ blocks
6 blocks across, 7 blocks down;
42 blocks
2″ border between blocks

This design requires a great deal of accurate cutting and sewing, and so is not for beginners. Piece the pattern in four-inch sections. The four corner sections and the center section consist of Units 1 and 2; the four remaining sections consist of Units 3 and 4. When all nine sections are pieced, set them together to form the block.

Use soft solid colors and small prints: the colors and prints should be uniform throughout the quilt. For the borders, pick up a light color from the background of a predominant print.

This design looks best among antiques—

for instance, on a brass bed with a white eyelet dust ruffle with matching pillow shams. I have also seen the quilt in a room decorated in Oriental style, and it looked fabulous. In this setting, the dust ruffle should be a soft-colored antique satin.

The name of this quilt dates from the mid-1800s. It was common for quilts to be named for people—often the people who made them—and many patterns bear the name "grandmother." It was considered an honor for a family to have a quilt made for them by a grandmother, and they repaid the honor by naming the quilt for her.

WHEEL OF FORTUNE QUILT, 1880
Manchester, Maryland
Made by Sarah J. Hann

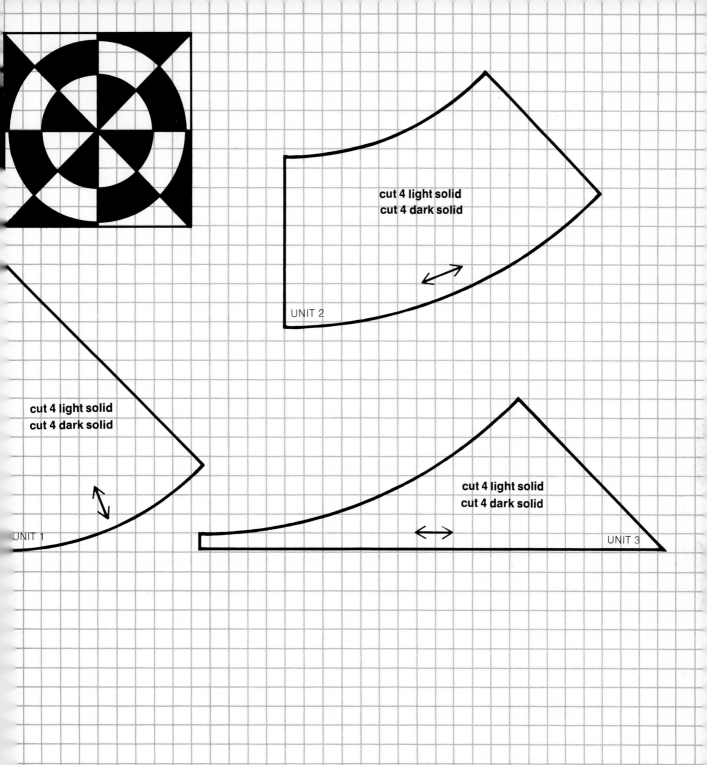

cut 4 light solid
cut 4 dark solid

UNIT 2

cut 4 light solid
cut 4 dark solid

UNIT 1

cut 4 light solid
cut 4 dark solid

UNIT 3

WHEEL OF FORTUNE QUILT

72″ x 92″
10″ blocks
6 blocks across, 8 blocks down;
48 blocks
Finished with three 2″ borders

Curves are difficult to execute well: don't attempt this pattern if you are a beginner. Piece all curves into their corresponding triangular sections before putting the units together as a finished block. Piece Units 2 and 3 first; then add Unit 1. Slash all curved seams so that the curves lie flat.

Bold solid colors are best for this quilt: red, white, and blue are a stunning combination. The borders should be the same colors as the blocks, and they should be arranged in the same color sequence as the block design, starting with the color in Unit 3 first.

This design goes well in modern decor; its optical quality fits with chrome and glass furniture. The pattern is excellent for a wall hanging.

Named in the 1930s, Wheel of Fortune is a variation of an older Pennsylvania Dutch pattern, the Buggy Wheel. It also resembles a pattern of the late 1800s called Wheel of Chance.

ODDS AND ENDS QUILT, 1900
Manchester, Maryland
Made by Sarah J. Hann

74

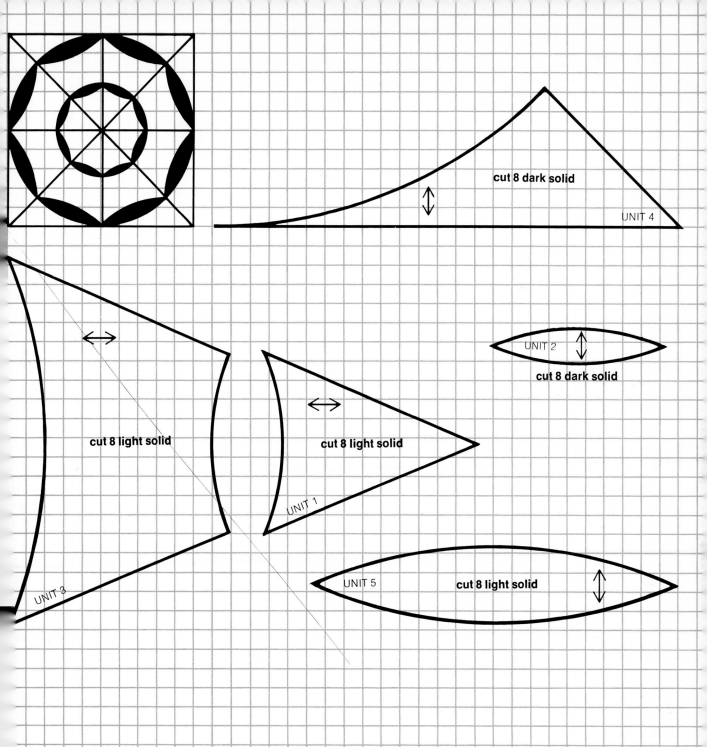

cut 8 dark solid

UNIT 4

cut 8 light solid

UNIT 2

cut 8 dark solid

cut 8 light solid

UNIT 1

UNIT 3

UNIT 5 cut 8 light solid

ODDS AND ENDS QUILT

82" x 96"

12" blocks

6 blocks across, 7 blocks down;

42 blocks

2" border between blocks

This is a difficult pattern to piece because of the complicated curves. It is not recommended for beginners, nor is it recommended for machine sewing. It should be pieced in eight triangular sections, each consisting of a set of five units, starting with Unit 1 and working outward. When all eight sections have been pieced, put the design together. Slash all curved seams so that they will lie flat.

Make Odds and Ends with solid colors. White muslin is a good choice for the light color. Prints do not enhance this design at all.

This quilt goes best with modern decor. Frame individual blocks or put several together for a wall hanging.

This design was named in the late 1800s. It has been said that it is not a beautiful design and that it was made only by people who could not afford fine fabric; supposedly coarsely woven fabric was used, giving the quilts a rugged, unpolished look. Yet, this design was found in the most gracious of homes in later years, and today we would surely judge it beautiful.

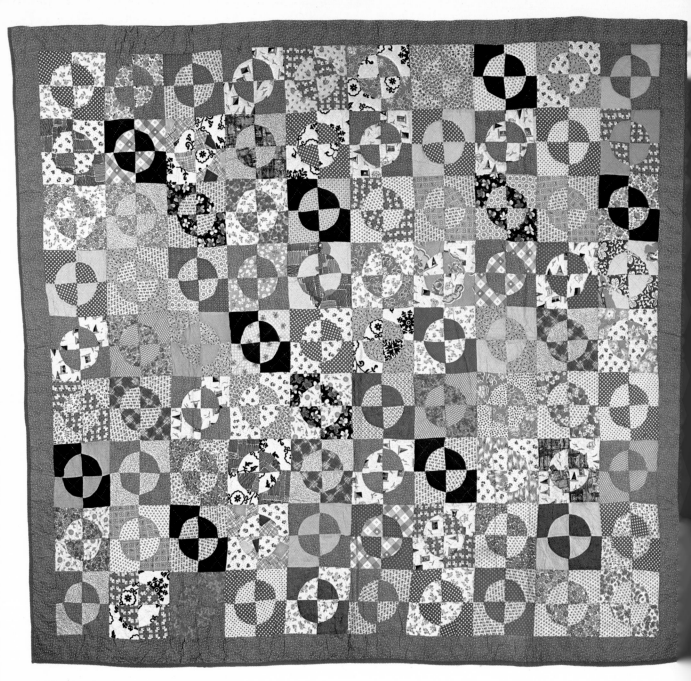

ROB PETER TO PAY PAUL QUILT, 1890
Manchester, Maryland
Made by Sarah J. Hann

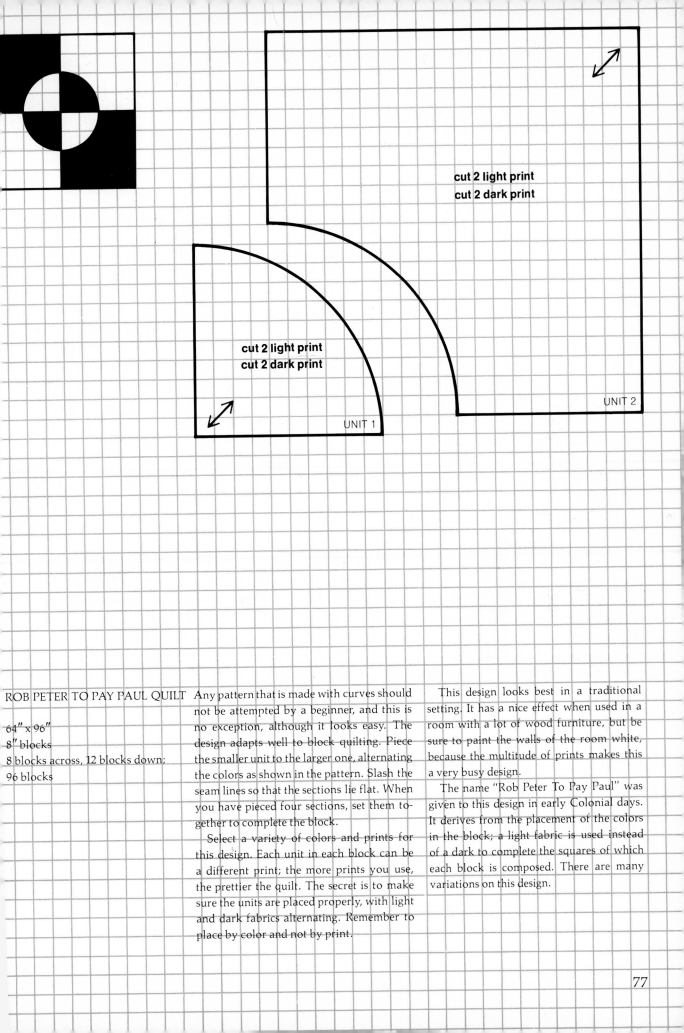

cut 2 light print
cut 2 dark print

cut 2 light print
cut 2 dark print

UNIT 1

UNIT 2

ROB PETER TO PAY PAUL QUILT

64" x 96"
8" blocks
8 blocks across, 12 blocks down;
96 blocks

Any pattern that is made with curves should not be attempted by a beginner, and this is no exception, although it looks easy. The design adapts well to block quilting. Piece the smaller unit to the larger one, alternating the colors as shown in the pattern. Slash the seam lines so that the sections lie flat. When you have pieced four sections, set them together to complete the block.

Select a variety of colors and prints for this design. Each unit in each block can be a different print; the more prints you use, the prettier the quilt. The secret is to make sure the units are placed properly, with light and dark fabrics alternating. Remember to place by color and not by print.

This design looks best in a traditional setting. It has a nice effect when used in a room with a lot of wood furniture, but be sure to paint the walls of the room white, because the multitude of prints makes this a very busy design.

The name "Rob Peter To Pay Paul" was given to this design in early Colonial days. It derives from the placement of the colors in the block; a light fabric is used instead of a dark to complete the squares of which each block is composed. There are many variations on this design.

LOG CABIN QUILT, 1850
Salt Lake City, Utah
Author's Collection

78

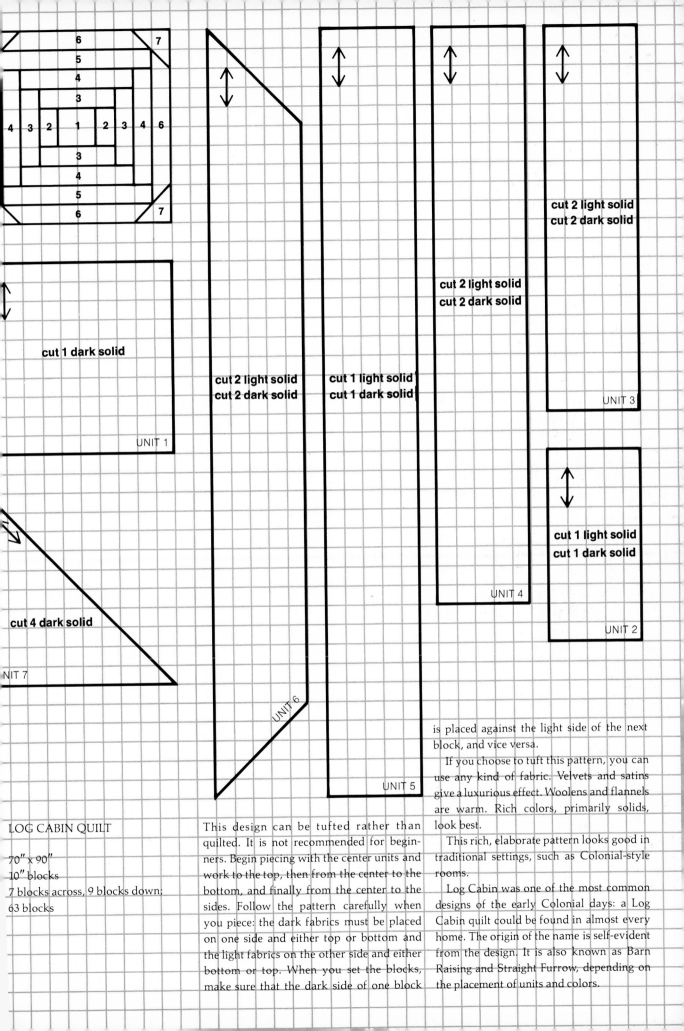

cut 2 light solid
cut 2 dark solid

UNIT 3

cut 2 light solid
cut 2 dark solid

cut 1 dark solid

cut 2 light solid
cut 2 dark solid

cut 1 light solid
cut 1 dark solid

UNIT 1

cut 1 light solid
cut 1 dark solid

UNIT 4

cut 4 dark solid

UNIT 2

NIT 7

UNIT 6

UNIT 5

LOG CABIN QUILT

70″ x 90″
10″ blocks
7 blocks across, 9 blocks down;
63 blocks

This design can be tufted rather than quilted. It is not recommended for beginners. Begin piecing with the center units and work to the top, then from the center to the bottom, and finally from the center to the sides. Follow the pattern carefully when you piece: the dark fabrics must be placed on one side and either top or bottom and the light fabrics on the other side and either bottom or top. When you set the blocks, make sure that the dark side of one block is placed against the light side of the next block, and vice versa.

If you choose to tuft this pattern, you can use any kind of fabric. Velvets and satins give a luxurious effect. Woolens and flannels are warm. Rich colors, primarily solids, look best.

This rich, elaborate pattern looks good in traditional settings, such as Colonial-style rooms.

Log Cabin was one of the most common designs of the early Colonial days: a Log Cabin quilt could be found in almost every home. The origin of the name is self-evident from the design. It is also known as Barn Raising and Straight Furrow, depending on the placement of units and colors.

NINE PATCH, 1850
Manchester, Maryland
(Author's Collection)

80

7.

THE CARE OF QUILTS

Always remember and respect the hours of work that went into the making of a quilt. To assure long life for your quilt, proper care is essential.

To wash a quilt, use cold water and a mild detergent. Run the machine on a short cycle. To keep the colors bright, add half a cup of white vinegar to the wash cycle.

The ideal way to dry a quilt is to hang it on a line out-of-doors. The sun freshens a quilt as nothing else can. If you must use a dryer, tumble dry with cool air. *Never* press a quilt with an iron.

Although it is an expensive proposition, the best method of cleaning a quilt is French hand cleaning. Never put your quilt in the hands of regular drycleaners, as the quilting stitches will be damaged by the drycleaning process.

Tufted comforters that are in constant use should be aired out often to keep their body and life. A comforter filled with down or kapok cannot be washed. It should be drycleaned every six months, and it should be aired out weekly. Each morning it should be fluffed. Proper care of this type will assure years of wear.

When it is not in use, store your quilt on a hanger in a closet that is not crowded, in a cedar chest, or in a cardboard box, but never in plastic wrappers. A quilt must be allowed to breathe at all times.

When you take a quilt out of storage, air it out. Lay it on the grass and let the sun penetrate it, or tumble it in a cool dryer for a short time. Never fold a quilt the same way day after day. If a quilt is stored folded, refold it at least twice a month. These simple measures assure fewer crease lines and a perfect shape for years.

Quilt small articles on a mir
frame like this one. The desig
illustrated is an Irish Chai
(Sample by Mauve Greenbaur

82

8.

OTHER USES OF PATCHWORK

Whether in clothing or accessories, potholders or draperies, patchwork has a personality that gives warmth to the hostess and her home. Items made from patchwork make lovely, personal gifts that will be treasured by the receiver.

Save scraps from quilts to use in the making of small articles. When you have decided what to make, choose patterns and colors carefully, as you would for a quilt.

All small patchwork items should be pieced and quilted to size. Be accurate in your measurements of items to be made so that you will not have waste. It is in such waste that small articles become expensive, and unnecessarily so. Piece the top as you would a quilt top, using whatever method—frame, block, or machine—you have found to be most comfortable.

The quilting of a small article such as a pillow can be done on a mini-frame of 1" x 2" lumber and assembled with C-clamps as for a coverlet. A 24"-square frame may be adjusted to any smaller size you need.

Instead of basting the backing to the mini-frame, you can use thumbtacks. Lay the batting and top the same as for a quilt, and proceed with drawing of the quilting design as described in Chapter 5. The finishing will depend on the item.

Potholders make good small gifts
and are great practice pieces for
the beginning quilter. These designs are Jacob's Ladder and the
Dresden Plate. (Blocks by Mauve
Greenbaum)

potholders

A small but good gift for the kitchen, as well as a good practice piece for beginners, potholders are very simple to make. A single ten-inch block with a full patchwork design is the best choice. Finish with or without a binding, and add a loop for hanging, or stuff a small magnet within the binding. The finishing of a potholder is the same, on a small scale, as the finishing of a quilt.

Infinite variations on the same basic unit shapes: a nice set of potholders. These all have borders and loops for hanging. (Samples by Mauve Greenbaum)

place mats

Patchwork place mats are as easy to assemble as potholders and add a pleasing touch to table settings. They can be made to any specification. An ideal size, however, consists of a sixteen-inch square made up of four eight-inch blocks. To add a special richness of effect to a set, make each mat a different design. Finish as you would a quilt.

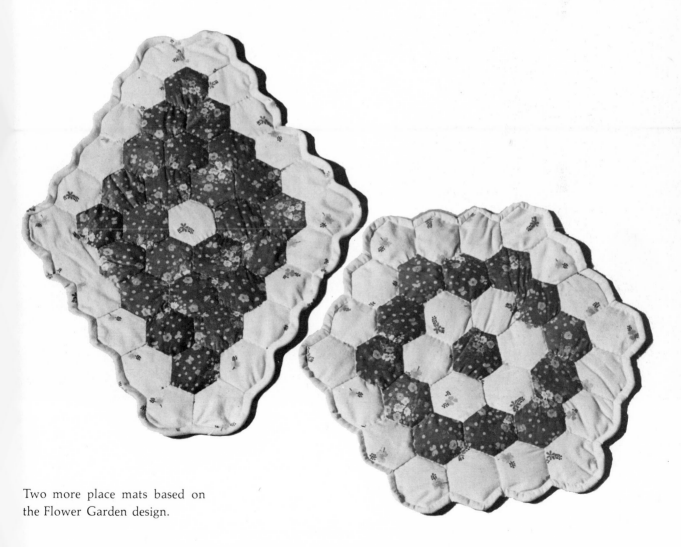

Two more place mats based on the Flower Garden design.

An assortment of patchwork
pillows. (Samples by Mauve
Greenbaum)

pillows

Any patchwork pattern and any size block can be used in making pillows. You can make a nice reversible pillow by using a different design for each side. Do not finish the edges of the quilted block. Sew the block and the backing together on the wrong sides, leaving an opening so you can pull the pillow through to the right side. Stuff the pillow and sew the open seam with a whip stitch.

Two pillows that are versions of the Jacob's Ladder design. (Samples by Mauve Greenbaum)

patchwork in home furnishings

Quiltmaking can be used imaginatively in home furnishings such as drapes, upholstery fabric for chairs and couches, and laminated table tops.

A room becomes handsomely warm with a window treatment of patchwork. In draperies and curtains, the patchwork should not be quilted, but the valances should be quilted. Piece the patchwork fabric needed for the drapes, allowing enough fabric for pleating. Line the drapes with a fabric that will keep out the sun to prevent fading. Many department stores carry ready-made pinch pleating that can be used for easy pleating. Quilt the valances and attach them to a cornice or a rod.

Be sure to take accurate measurements of furniture to be covered, and allow enough quilted fabric for seams and overhangs. Upholstering is a job for expert sewers, but the results are well worth the effort.

air upholstered with patchwork. (Courtesy of The Landmark, Great Neck, New York)

A table top laminated with patchwork provides a colorful accent in any room. Make a pieced top to the exact size of the table top. Quilt, depending on the size, on a mini-frame or a larger frame. Finish the edges. Using a vinyl wallpaper adhesive or glue, spread a thin coat evenly over the back of the fabric and set into place on the table top. With a sharp razor, take off the excess fabric. You can then coat the fabric with varnish or cover it with glass to ensure that the patchwork will not be stained.

patchwork for walls

Finished quilts add color and life to any room—wall hangings: attach them to a decorative rod. One or more blocks can also be framed and hung in any room of the home.

A patchwork tennis dress and racquet cover. (Made by the author)

patchwork in fashion

Patchwork can spruce up any wardrobe—a man's or a woman's. Any article of clothing can be made from patchwork, from skirts and pants to vests and ties, and the effect can be casual or very elegant.

Use an ordinary pattern for the garment, but add at least one extra yard to the amount of fabric required in the pattern. This gives you enough fabric to match your seams. Break the yardage estimate of the pattern down to the total amounts of fabric needed for piecing. Select a patchwork design that will suit the item to be made. If you do not plan to quilt the fabric, you can use velvets and other fine fabrics. Machine piecing is recommended for clothing.

Garments made of quilted fabrics do not need linings or interfacings. If you do not quilt, however, the patchwork must be lined. Using the pattern, cut out the lining according to the directions for fabrics with a nap. Baste the lining in place before sewing and check that all seams match and meet properly. Finish according to pattern.

patchwork skirt made of satin an elegant outfit for entertain-g. (Made by Mamie Galt)

LIST OF SUPPLIERS

Batting:	Stearns and Foster Company Cincinnati, Ohio 45215
Printed Muslin:	Stanley Looms 1411 Broadway New York, New York 10018
Cotton Information:	Cotton Incorporated 1370 Avenue of the Americas New York, New York 10019
Quilting Frames:	Sears, Roebuck and Company Catalogue Divisions
Quilting Needles and Thread:	Coats and Clark 430 Park Avenue New York, New York 10022
Machine Quilting:	Wrightway Quilting 5280 North Broadway Denver, Colorado 80216